Long Island, New York

Published By JLE Press
Long Island, New York
E-Mail: JLEpress2016@yahoo.com

Printed in the United States of America

Prologue

When hearing the word "casualty", one tends to attribute it to the negative aspect of war. Divorce may not involve physical weaponry such as guns and tanks, but its emotional impact can maim or injure an entire family just the same. The combatants fight in bedrooms, they fight in living rooms, sometimes they fight in view of the unknowing public, until they ultimately take their fight to the courtrooms. These long, tedious and emotional battles can rage on for months, even years. The costs are staggering, both in the wallet and in the heart. Hatred and animosities are forever forged, bitterness and apathy become commonplace, all to hold on to what little you have left or to capture as much treasure as you can. One side may eventually claim victory, but the reality of it all is that in The Game of War, as it applies to divorce, there is never a single victor. The spouses, who have borne the entire toll, their children, who suffer emotional confusion as they watch their families fall apart, and the collateral damage which reaches far beyond the immediate family; those relationships transformed or lost forever. The Casualties of Divorce offers a front row seat to the turmoil endured by all when two adults decide to end their marriage, for whatever reason. The book explores the different perspectives and experiences as told by dozens of persons who have proverbially "walked the walk" amongst different degrees of separation. It is intended to provide the reader with the understanding that they are not alone, their feelings are valid and that *"This Too Shall Pass"*. Co-authored by three casualties of divorce, this book will enlighten those who are contemplating divorce and comfort those who have survived one.

For The Casualties...

The Casualties Of Divorce

Written by:
Vincent Casale
Jayson Cole
Thomas J. Billotti, Ph.D

Cover Design:
CreativeFX
Graphic Design

The Pit of My Stomach

"But if the unbeliever leaves, let it be so. The brother or the sister is not bound in such circumstances; God has called us to live in peace."
~1 Corinthians 7:15

The darkness of divorce realizes the illusion of the age old vows. Love, honor, cherish, through good times and through bad.

The following stories are told from the viewpoints of men and women who have suffered the consequences of divorce and the break of their nuclear family. No matter who is involved, the decisions that led to their divorce, right or wrong, they harbor similar emotions regarding the rollercoaster ride of doubt, guilt, anger, and humiliation, the pain of separation from one's children and the abysmal feeling of marginalization. It is the children who suffer the initial shock and fear of divorce followed by feeling hopelessly rejected by the parent who leaves the home, no matter how hard that parent tries to reassure the children. The parent child bond becomes damaged from this pain and the greatly reduced contact with the "visiting" parent exerts a death grip on the relationship. This negates any guidance or influence that parent had with the children prior to the divorce. Once the visiting parent becomes marginalized in the children's lives, the children become increasingly hostile and distant and complete the cycle by ultimately rejecting the parent. But the pain in the pits of the children's stomachs may continue indefinitely as they experience unforeseen consequences of the damaged parent-child bond, such as a lifetime of fearing abandonment, difficulty trusting others, problems with male or female authority figures. Finally, in many circumstances comes the financial ruin. Attorney fees, court fees, and a mountain of small print that couldn't possibly be deciphered by a layman. The co-authors of this journal spent countless hours interviewing men and women.

They listened intently to all those befriended professionally and through six degrees of separation, outside of the rule, in bars and restaurants, and in some cases polite family barbeques.

One of the three authors is a practicing psychologist who has treated victims of divorce for over thirty years. He has created "composite cases" to protect the identities of his clients.

Dr. Billotti makes practical and sensible recommendations in a later chapter in the hope of relieving some of the suffering and minimizing the negative impact of divorce on children in the future. We are all hopeful that matrimonial judges, lawyers and parents who will be divorcing will give careful consideration to these recommendations, and that they may encourage residential custody and visitation agreements that are more protective of the children's long term emotional health.

The three authors were in agreement that the text would not be a disparagement of men or women. None have any affiliation with the father's rights movement although our roles and influence as fathers have been greatly diminished due to divorce. With the blowing winds of divorce, which were thrust upon them, the contributors answered questions, as it is human nature, for all to be contradictory and redundant. We have tried our best to limit that. This is not a bash fest, rather a document recounting the relentless casualties a divorce can cause. There is the magic and element of surprise when interviewing those that could be hit with any question even if that person decides it is not printable. One of the subjects confessed to us that he actually prayed for his wife. He wanted her to do well because he believed if she had a good life, then so too would his children. He decided to inform his God that he would rather his wife live a longer life than he. He had visited church, sat in a pew, and explained to his God that he truly loved his wife, and that his love for her was like a first love that lasted the longest. He described how he became overwrought with emotion and acknowledged to his almighty that he knew when his life was off kilter. In his past he had come to pray, and admitted the praying always seemed to cease when things were going well. He would come back this time he promised. If only...

On one such visit he thought the church was empty, and when he got up to leave, a middle-aged woman, who apparently noticed his emotion, was just rising from a far away pew. "Are you OK?" she asked.

He was tempted to hug her and say, "No, I'm not, please talk to me. Please help me figure out the tide of my life. It is ebbing away and I can't stop it!" Instead, he wiped the wetness encompassing his eyes and told the woman he was fine and thanked her for asking.

The interviews and the sacraments have ended and now begins the task of deciphering the consequences, or casualties, thus picking up the pieces. Some readers might not have sympathy for our second character, Chris. But his pseudonym agreed for an interview, to let us know that, although it was mostly his doing in wanting out of his marriage, it didn't negate the fact that he was hurting as much as any other divorcee. The reader will acknowledge that Chris was not looking for a pity party during or after the interview. We knew he would be an important part of the conversation. In fact, none of the subjects wanted to attract any sympathy.

From the beginning of the sacred wedding vows, what person does not begin the journey of marriage with the hope that there exists a lifetime of love, friendship and trust from the human being they expect to walk through life with.

Dreams forsaken, fairy tales gone haywire. Resentments from the smallest of issues, like leaving a toilet seat lifted, snacking on a dessert without asking the other if they would like a taste, dirty clothes left everywhere, dishes lingering in a messy sink, to the long periods of silence and the suffering of infidelity.

It is the authors' belief, any individual with a soul, will encounter a wide array of physical, emotional and psychological issues as they navigate the termination of their marriage and the separation from their children. Each person handles these issues differently from the next and no one person is ever credited with addressing them the "right" way or chastised for dealing with them the "wrong" way. It is also the authors' intentions to recognize and explain these many facets by the use of fictional characters derived from our numerous interviews to illustrate the wide range of feelings and emotions that one may or may not experience through this most difficult process.

What you will read are the stories and the pain of many different people; people whose lives have been forever altered by the devastation of divorce. The authors have acknowledged and validated their experiences and piecemealed the issues that they faced and presented them collectively within the stories of a few composite characters; all with the intention of allowing the reader to feel the similarities of those who confront this fate.

Michael's Story

"Whatever gets you through the night"
~Francis Albert

It was early spring when I interviewed Michael. He is of medium height, 54 years of age and well groomed. Michael is in no way an intimidating figure but I still felt a little nerdy in my checkered shirt while he wore a black t-shirt under a light black leather jacket. He ordered a couple of lattes at the counter. He insisted on paying. Though we have bonded socially a number of times, I could immediately detect his nervousness about going on the record about his impending divorce from his wife of twenty two years. We decided on a corner table at Barnes and Noble, a place he called his favorite hangout. A place he could find some semblance of peace by skimming through the many books. "Like a church to me sometimes," he said. "I used to bring my children here. What a joy it was, watching them pick out books..." *(Can I get two books dad?)*.

Though visibly tired, Michael's eyes are a startling blue. He is humble and does not realize their power. He kind of reminded me of myself, not only physically but also possessing a curious nature.

Decisively, my co-authors and I agreed not to hold back

even the most personal of questions. The interviewees, trusting us, agreed. Still there was always the element of surprise, and it was understood if a question or answer was too emotional, then naturally we would ease up. Yet, I was confidant non-responses would be few and far between. I began after the usual salutations.

"Are you up to this buddy? I mean really?" I asked.

"Shoot away Vince. I'll do my best."

We both laughed somewhat nervous.

"Here we go," I said. I was hoping my own nerves would survive and the ink on my paper wouldn't be just a blur.

"Mike, you have been separated about ten months?" I asked.

"About that. Unfortunately, my pain still circles like a never-ending black cloud. So this, though we have had many conversations, is still going to be rough for me."

I knew but I said nothing as he already had the look of a man trying to catch up to his memory. Sometimes when Michael is sitting he can't sit still, his legs will vibrate up and down. This was one of those times.

He continued. "My anxiety is still high...thought I was going to have a heart attack in the beginning...when I left, when we separated...had to pull my car over to the side of the road." He was contemplating more, so I let it ride. "My family thinks I should have been over her six months ago, whereas for me I almost wish I had had a heart attack, full blown, massive and quick."

He snapped his fingers and he wasn't smiling. "That's so ridiculous," I replied. "A marriage with three children and twenty-two years, I don't think it's so easy to get over. And as far as the heart attack you will come to see that that is also ridiculous."

"My wife seems to appear more insensitive in post separation than the events leading up to it." Michael lifted his latte and blew into the steaming cup. "Again my whole support system, friends, family, even my therapist believe that I don't really love my wife. That I'm just pining over something I can't have...What nobody understands is, all through my bitching and moaning I never uttered the words that I don't love my wife."

I asked, "Why then did you not fight harder to hold your marriage together?"

"I ran out of steam. I admit, it got to the point where I just wanted out, although believe me, I really in retrospect believe I was iced out."

Michael exhaled and explained to me he believed his wife made a calculated move to push him out, thus he would be blamed for leaving. She would be disavowed of any responsibility. "As if it were an agenda," he said. He waved his hand up and down. "Going from offense to defense. Mathematical." His voice had trailed off and he left it at that. "I didn't have any fight left Vin. We promised to respect each other, communicate, make love more often...We almost split five years ago. In all that time we just selfishly didn't get it." Michael looked into his cup seemingly dejected.

"And?" I said.

"We tried therapy...just didn't work. There was no fight left in her either...it began to crumble again two years ago. Finally, when I asked out, she agreed immediately." Michael turned looking at the coffee counter as to not look me in the eye.

"You sure there wasn't infidelity?" I asked.

"Not on my part. I'm pretty certain not on hers either."

He sighed looked at me with squinting sad eyes, projecting a pain he has yet to shed. "But then again, the husband is the last to know. Funny thing is even if there was on her part, or when the next guy does enter the picture; she's going to have to make love or have sex.
She can't say no because she's tired or he's not showing enough affection, you know the usual shit woman will use so as not to look wrong. She has to try and communicate and respect with a greater attempt. Reality, no one wants another person's drama." Michael took a breath after a momentary but contained tirade.
"That's not your problem anymore," I said.

His pain palpable, he ceased conversation in this regard. "Look at all these books around us," Michael continued, his eyes sweeping the room. "Classics, psychology references, and self-help books that couldn't help a friggin' moron. I've chosen to read a lot of books with happy endings of late. Wishful thinking...Let's face it; happy endings are only in books and movies. I try remembering my wife one afternoon when she wore a yellow sundress and I thought her so beautiful. Do you think she ever thought that seeing me in any form? Well that can only be replayed in a movie."

"Nothing wrong with romance. Sometimes there are happy endings," I said. "Could it be you just grew apart?"

The comment seemed to agitate him. "You know," Michael said. "You sound like my previous therapist. He told me that he believed all marriages have a shelf life. That kind of pissed me off. Through thick and thin." He made the quote sign with his fingers... "My Aunt and Uncle they were married sixty-five years."

"Different times," I reiterated.

He referred back to memory. "It was an inconceivable

14

notion, a strange feeling of discomfort to not even hold hands anymore. Didn't go on vacations, just her and me. No more interest in each other's lives." Michael just looked around, nowhere in particular. "Though I was very proud of her career, I didn't know too much about it. Computer, numbers. She never asked me how my day went. She actually criticized that I worked in a country club precinct as if there were never any danger. She knew I loved books, as she did, and movies, but not enough to talk about them; not lately anyway. I guess we both got bored and didn't let our happier times fight it off..." Michael kind of glazed over.

"Yet I remember our last dinner and a movie, a real date night. She used to like to put her legs up around mine in the theater...

"Now as I watch television alone I no longer watch the TV shows we used to sit on the couch and watch together. I don't give a shit about those characters anymore."

"Grew apart." I was sorry as soon as the words came out of my mouth.

"Again with that?" he said. I turned away as he pointed his finger at me. "Growing apart. What does that even mean? Is it really possible to begin with, to think that people don't have moments of growing apart? Aren't they supposed to tie it back together?"

I let it lie for now as we sipped our lattes. My glasses fogged from the steam in the cup as I sniffed the cinnamon. I wanted him to realize that yes people do definitely grow apart and sometimes they just cannot put the pieces back together. He didn't want to hear that now, waving his hand as if to say get lost. I realized similar questions would run through all the interviews, with our friends and their encounters with disappointment. But our hope was to get them to release some of their angst. Questions and answers of repeated doubt, boredom, distance, as if we were all agents of the natural progression in marriages. I for one felt these men also needed to realize that it does take two to tango. When the marriage dissolves because of the lack of communication no one person should carry the weight on their shoulders.

Michael's voice dropped to almost a whisper. "Maybe I miss my old life because it's gone. Maybe my reservations are because of the loss of my family as a nucleus, missing my children and being unable to monitor their joys and sadness on a daily basis. It's so hurtful...I immediately missed that place I could call home. It was a safe haven, my family and I bonded together from the outside world, sheltering us in some way. Don't get me wrong. I am well aware that even if I were still home that wouldn't mean the kids wouldn't be moody or wouldn't want anything to do with me on any given day. After all they are teens. *(Dad, I am not going to discuss my friends with you)*. Still, it just feels different."

Clearly there were some realities in his life. Strangely, I again became nervous. Although I knew my subject socially, we had talked about life, work and interests; I now felt a sense of intrusion.

We discussed what we were aiming for. Of course I've heard many of these answers during conversations but they still were very compelling as I took pen to hand. We talked of women. Michael joked, "An animal of a different color. Doesn't matter what social background or religion they come from. Doesn't matter."

He laughed when I assured him females felt the same about us.

Now, as I believed the sincerity of this individual and his seemingly negative outlook, my heart really went out to him. However as sad as the episode was he still has three beautiful children to hold in his heart for the rest of his life, something I knew without any reservations he would come to realize.

Michael continued as I looked directly at him. Maybe he would feel he had a true and honest friend. Thankfully my glasses acted as somewhat of a shield against my obvious concern. I guess it's true that most men still will attempt to hide their emotions. "OCD doubt I guess," he said. "You know I'm more mentally obsessive than the next guy."

"No didn't know that," I said. I rubbed my hands together.

"You mean you are obsessed with washing your hands?" I was smiling.

"Obsessions; Thoughts of doubt, over and over. The problem with OCD is that failure is a terrible option to think about over and over again. You know my middle name is Thomas. Maybe that should have been my first name, "Doubting Thomas.""

Michael always had some kind of analogy. I really didn't know who he would ultimately compare himself to. I was hoping he would just be himself. It came to me and I remembered meeting a childhood friend of Michael's when we were out in a local Queens tavern. Nice guy, squat with a thick neck and a thick head of hair that I was jealous of. After a few beers with his buddy, realizing I could be trusted, he told me Michael was his best friend from when they were kids. Then he said, sadly, as if he already knew Michael's fate, "My buddy has always been that 'grass is greener on the other side guy.' Not in any mean sort of way. He is just always searching for something that might not even be there."

Michael again explained that of course he missed his children. Thankfully they had each other. *(When is dad coming home?).*

However, if that was the only symptom of regret why was it that when he laid his head down on his pillow at night, every sleepless night, he woke in the morning and it was she, his ex-wife that occupied his mind. She was right there in front of him. He remembered when they first met. She told him she was immediately attracted to him. His warm blue eyes, his hair slicked back, way before it turned white. She told him later that she loved his conversations when they talked of books. She loved historical novels, and he enjoyed mostly pulp. Conversations long gone.

The good times are what many couples remember. Perhaps because the good thoughts gave validation and reassurance that we didn't make a mistake in the first place.

He pressed on. "Before we were married and I had my apartment I tried hammering a nail in the wall to hang a picture. I kept making the hole bigger and bigger, as I was never one for handy type work... I became so frustrated I threw the nail on the floor and stated, 'I keel you.' Well my crazy mispronunciation had her rolling with laughter so genuine that it was infectious. It was a hysterical moment. We both laughed for what seemed like an hour. Our stomachs were hurting we laughed so much. Well I was never a hammer and a nail type of guy."

He continued his issue of good times. Their honeymoon, Michael told me, other than dehydrating there were some lasting beautiful moments. "We wrapped our bodies around each other in that clear blue water," he recalled.

Then the busy years: The kid years, school calendars (school's okay I guess), work calendars, etc. Suddenly, they couldn't remember the last time they smiled at each other, not aware that the distance between them had just sneaked up on them like a sickness.

Michael went outside to smoke a cigarette. I went and grabbed two more lattes. When he returned he seemed anxious again as if he couldn't wait to get something off his chest.

He apologized for his nicotine habit. Nasty habit, he admitted. *(Dad, you and mom both need to quit)*. Michael was now smoking two packs a day. But other than I hoped he wouldn't get cancer it didn't bother me in the least. "You know I used to think all those bullshit dreams that actors have in soap operas or movies couldn't possibly be real dreaming of current events as if reliving them. Anyway, the craziest dream happened to me. I was laying on my right side and in my dream my wife was behind me with her arms around me. I turned around to look, it was her." Michael closed his own arms around himself as he explained. He spoke as if she were illuminated in the dark. "Her hair was tousled from her pillow, her skin soft, I smelled her. When I woke I instantly looked around, instantly noticed there wasn't anyone behind me. It made me want to go back to sleep and recapture whatever was left of that dream.

"Anyway Vince, thank God the kids are teens now and there is not the extra stress of a custody battle. That scenario would have flat out drove me insane... It's still hard though. Sure their love is unconditional. But they could be a pain sometimes. Moody. I guess it affects me more because I don't live at home." *(We love you but you don't have to try and see us every other day. Once a week of quality time is okay)*.

"That's where I have to really learn to compartmentalize. I feel sometimes they go out with me to go through the motions; it sometimes seems they really don't want to be there with me. But if I were home it would be the same. They are teens and they do have a social calendar. When I was a teen I wasn't thrilled about hanging out with my parents."

I certainly understood and we both smiled at the reality of teenagers. "But I refuse to be my father. I will not ruin the relationship I have with my kids because I couldn't face the woman I love!" Michael flipped open his phone to the photo gallery, pictures of his kids. "So beautiful, like their mother."

He smiled at the generosity he awarded his wife. "I will give them more than a handful of memories."

I leaned over the small round table and squeezed his arm.

"They are indeed beautiful. You're a good guy Mike, of that I have no doubt." Suddenly he welled up. I saw the moisture on the corner of his eyes. I said nothing.

"I'll never forget," he said. His lips began to quiver. "I'll never for the rest of my life forgets the looks on their faces when we told them..." *(Can we go upstairs now?)* He wiped the sides of his face with a napkin without embarrassment. Then he folded it over his mouth. He would later tell me that he was ready to burst into tears. I knew the memory of those kids; dejection in their faces would remain with him forever like ink on a paper.

It had all changed in that moment. The fabric of the entire family was switching gears.

There would be no more family gatherings together. There would be separate birthday parties, graduation parties, and vacations. The children would visit with respective families on both sides only without both parents.

The image of one daughter's graduation where he had to say goodbye to his family in the parking lot, still haunted him. Michael would find himself driving alone for hours with terribly sad music playing on the radio. He noticed that a whole baseball season had gone by and he paid little attention to a sport he loved. And if not for his family, his siblings and his mother, waking up Christmas morning

(Mom, Dad, hurry, look what Santa brought me!) would have crushed him for life. It was a horrible holiday season. He had to turn his head in the mall when he saw all the children waiting in line to jump onto Santa's lap. Reminding himself that he once was a part of this world had caused him to breath heavier than usual.

"If someone would have approached me in the mall they would surely have asked me if I was alright. At my age someone for sure would have thought I was having a heart attack...Anytime I see children the past haunts me. I immediately recall birthdays and park swings and preschool and grammar school, *Toys r Us*, their first puppy..."
(Oh, my god, he's soooo cute!) Michael put his head down, sighing and shaking from side to side.

"Let's pick this up another day Mike. There is no time limit on this."

Michael agreed and I was glad because the emotional roller coaster had begun and every one of us were going to need a break from a journey that I was sure would take us to confusion, confession and hopefully enlightenments.

"Am I the first Guinea pig?" Michael joked.

"Yes I believe you are," I replied. "You did fine buddy. I believe you held up better than I would have."

Future discussions would not consist of his relationship with his father. We were going to relive the here and the now, the immediate past. But I did know his parents' divorce made him feel like even more than a failure. One thing I was sure of was that he was a better father to his kids than his father would have imagined. Michael was not going to divorce his children.

Once I climbed into my car I looked over at Mike. He was sitting behind the wheel of his car his shoulders slumped over the steering wheel, with his arm hanging out the window, cigarette in his left hand. I pushed my glasses up, turned my engine over. I left with Michael still sitting there. We both had a lot to ponder.

I thought a diner would be a good place to continue. Michael had a few days to re-group and was now eager. His wish was to repair his lonely soul. To admit his mistakes, he called temporary rusting of the brain, mind blindness. We sat in the rear of the diner and were able to look out at a wet Hempstead Turnpike in Bethpage where a flow of traffic lined the three lanes. The day was reflective of the subject matter.

The world stops for no one, I thought strangely. Amass all of one individual's pain there is still the days that leave that bad taste in your mouth. Rainy days and days when traffic and rude people test those even with high regarded patience. Toothaches, colds, flat tires, paper cuts, spilling a cup of coffee, extended family issues, etc., etc. Nothing stops to allow those hurt to have the time to unwind. Well that's my psych lesson for the day.

Michael apologized for giving up at the previous meeting but I assured him there was no time limit. I just wanted him to be alright and as free from anxiety as he possibly could.

I ordered a burger deluxe and coffee. Michael relented telling me coffee was enough for now. He said he didn't have much of an appetite. "I couldn't eat a chicken nugget," he said. I laughed but was afraid that it was our conversation that would destroy his appetite.

He excused himself immediately going out for that cigarette. I was surprised, for a man who smoked frequently he did not have a smoker's cough.

When he returned he dove right into the subject. "I think our last meeting was kind of therapeutic."

"I'm glad Mike. Maybe it will wind up that way for all of

us."

"I don't want to talk sports or entertainment. Small formality chit chats. We have plenty of time for that another time," he said. "I want to try and purge myself without too many tears."

I agreed, and without mentioning his childhood or the failures of his father, we dove back into the matter at hand. "Well then," I said. "Have you gotten laid lately?" It broke the ice because he laughed.

"Vince, would you believe I just don't give a shit right now about a relationship. It's been almost a year and I don't care. My friends think it very strange. 'Get your rocks off,' they tell me. But..."

Michael didn't want love certainly but he needed to feel some kind of connection, or affection. He said he didn't want to use anyone on a level of pure sex. He wanted to at least wake up to someone he could spend more than two minutes with. Still I couldn't help thinking he was being coy with me. I knew he had been on a couple of wild vacations since his separation.

"It's sick but I feel maybe if I don't use anyone or maybe if I abstain, then she will…maybe she will wait and not get the urge to sleep with just anyone."

Unfortunately, I had to remind Michael of something he already knew, life just does not work that way. That she, his wife, is naturally going to be drawn to some kind of love no matter how misguided. I didn't want to say, but sometimes when a woman is done with her man, she remains done. I knew my friend had no illusions but somewhere deep in his fantasies he longed for some kind of hope. But he also had a yearning for 2014 to be a much better year. He said he would try and embrace life. Enjoy the things that used to belong to him personally. Places he'd never been to with his soon to be ex, Europe for example.

Still his promise to treat himself better was questionable with the look of attachment he perpetuated.

Returning to our talk of future amore, he said, "I'm just not feeling it," Then... "Excuse me I need a smoke." If it gets him through the day, let him puff, for now at least. His voice sounded raspier over the months since I met him, but no cough...

I stayed on the sex thing. As serious as sex could be there was always those times it could draw a laugh, lighten things up. "Well pal, sooner or later you will get laid." At least I got a smile out of him. I really shouldn't have relived this question since I already got the hint not to ask it again. It was just one of those subjects he was not going to delve into or be forthright. Yet I was trying to go for the complete honesty package we were striving for, but this wasn't a perfect science.

"Getting laid for men of my age," Michael said, "is easier said than done. Let me take that back, getting laid with someone who doesn't annoy you is easier said than done. A man might have his baggage, but a woman lives with hers, and who really wants that nonsense. It's a vicious cycle for all involved. It's not a Brady Bunch scenario."

"Kind of harsh, don't you think?" I asked.

"Well maybe. But as I said, right now I don't give a shit."

I made one last attempt to pull something out of him that he didn't want to discuss. Any conversation about sex he might or might not have had during his separation. As a man I felt, of course he satisfied one urge. But who knows. He really never did discuss his sex life with me, except for the lack there of in his marriage. As honest as we were all supposed to be maybe there are some things left completely unsaid, like places to visit where hedonism was an amusement park for men. Still I mentioned such destinations and got a huge wicked smile out of him, as if he knew exactly what I was referring to. But our species did have a clever way of compartmentalizing such actions.

"Any more psychobabble?" He pointed then lifted his cup. I was cutting my burger in half the way I like to eat it and Michael shook his head. He told me that he preferred tearing full into it. "Actually I wish there had been a third party on my behalf, two-fold, someone that we knew mutually. Someone, perhaps a family member or a friend who could be a buffer so to speak, but it never happened. I became extremely suspicious. Maybe no one wanted to intervene because they knew something I didn't. Maybe those around me absolutely knew it was over. Maybe they even knew about a boyfriend. *(If you think mom has a boyfriend, she doesn't!)*.

"Secondly, I wish that I had fallen for someone, and then maybe my hurt wouldn't be so bad; a useful rebound to fill the void.

"You know right after the separation I selfishly needed to get away. Get out of dodge so to speak. I flew off to Florida for a fourteen-day vacation; the worst trip I had ever been on, bar none. Not to mention a huge waste of money!"

He was anxious to think back to those early days of escape, so I listened intently.

"I thought I would visit all these Facebook friends who live up and down the Florida beltway from north to south east to west. I had it all planned. I emailed friends mapped out where they lived and set off for a journey that I assumed would help me forget...First thing about anywhere you go never ever travel without a wing man. I drove a lonely path from Daytona through small shit towns, down to the west coast to Ft. Meyers and ending in Naples. Then I drove the hundred miles into south Florida. Not a bad ride but again, not a very delightful one either when you have no one to talk to, especially when you feel like total shit and suddenly feeling worse as the days went on. What a joke."

"Sunshine sounds like a good---"

"I just told you it was the worst trip of my life. Not in a million years was it a good trip. I had planned to see about eight friends. Saw only four. The rest had plans as if I were coming from around the corner."

"Well people can't---"

"I know, put their lives on hold. Anyway out of the four I enjoyed hanging out with two..."

"What were you looking for?" I asked.

"The male fantasy of course; meeting a beautiful woman on the beach. Her taking me in for a while...Or maybe like the bubble bath commercial I was just looking for something to take me away.

"All I got was a few photos of the beach." He laughed.

"There are some pictures where I had any person take a picture of me with blue water in the background. It looked as though I was on a vacation with a real somebody, not my pathetic self." He had texted pictures to his kids. *(Water looks beautiful dad).*

Michael had that look of stark realization as if he knew at that moment life was going to veer into some sort of hell.

"Yep, worst vacation and loneliest two weeks of my life. Thought I was going to die from loneliness. It was dreadful. Wound up in a dive titty bar one night. Shot pool with an old stripper, missing teeth. Five bucks a game; though I knew I would have to win because I would never get the money...I won. Another night, when I first got there, I was in Daytona...I was staying in some musty motel that had advertised these great prices, and know I know why. There was no way I was going to sleep. Across the street was the Harley Davidson strip mall. I had zero interest in Harley or its gear but I walked around that mall over and over. Not a soul around. I was so drunk I could barely walk and barely see. But nevertheless I walked around and around." Michael motioned circles with his fingers and he had a far away look.

"I could think though. And I thought over and over and over." And now as Michael described his ordeal as if he were reliving it he began to thrust his forefinger into his temple. "What the hell happened to me? So I stood against a wall and I must have smoked three cigarettes back to back. At that precise moment I wondered if there were even a God, but I looked up and asked him to forgive me anyway."

I felt terrible for this guy. Though divorced myself I could never imagine being 2000 miles from home, thinking and wondering about everything, experiencing grief by myself, just gut-wrenching.

"But there was nothing to forgive Mike. It was a separation. It was not a one-sided decision!"

He didn't reflect on my comment, instead...

"Well buddy," he said. "I guess it was just great expectations. It was sort of like Steinbeck's "Travels with Charley", when he went cross-country in an old truck with just his dog. Even Charlie wasn't enough to quell his loneliness.

"Well at least I had the funds. I don't know. Maybe I should consider myself lucky."

"You mean you realize that divorce will work out for you? You're coming to terms?"

"No, I mean there is always someone worse off." Michael told me of one of his close friends, a retired policeman, let's call him Harry. Harry was married for twenty-eight years. Sure he and his wife had the usual problems of disagreeing over just about everything. Like anyone else he was no angel. He fell into the trap where everything started to irritate him. I guess we all are guilty of taking things for granted. Anyway, Harry comes home from a second job, which had supplemented to pay extra bills and save for his children's college tuition.

Harry thinks nothing of it when he sees his wife on Facebook. "An old friend from high school," she tells him, without batting an eye.

"At least I didn't learn of any boyfriend. Not to sound melodramatic but that would have felt as if I were being ripped in half by wild horses," Michael said.

"God gives us what we can handle," I said. I didn't mention finance, but the one saving grace for Michael was that his wife made more money than he did so he wouldn't forever be bogged down with enormous payments.

"Yeah, God," he replied.

I bit into half my burger. I didn't want to appear bored but I was more interested in Michael's life rather than someone I didn't know. It was indeed more personal. In my profession I have heard these stories a thousand times. Yet his reflection on his friend was contagious and for a moment I thought about a fireman friend of mine who couldn't get over his wife. Didn't realize she was really done with him, so he would show up at the house over and over, until the woman took out a restraining order. Against advice he still went there. The last time was when his son told him on the phone, 'Dad, why are you stealing our college money!' Still couldn't believe she would have him arrested. He showed up at the door. "Are you fucking crazy telling the kids a thing like that." He certainly couldn't explain his own financial circumstances. Kids that live at home with their mother wouldn't understand and shouldn't have to. How do you explain to children that you need more money to live a decent life on your own? It's impossible because it will only sound selfish in their eyes.

So he violated a total of five orders of protections. Bottom line he spent a year wearing an orange jumpsuit in Nassau County lock- up. His family never even told him what college his son registered for. *(Why are you taking 50% percent dad. Don't we have to go to school?)*

Michael grabbed one of my fries, which made me hope he was feeling less anxious.

"Long story short," Michael continued. "Husband catches bored housewife on Facebook and phone texts. She admits to an affair. He's of course out of his mind. Not only emotionally but now he has to pay up, a wrecking ball, right through the white picket fence dream. What the hell should a man pay a woman for if she is the adulterer... house gone...car gone... college funds depleted on lawyers. In the end I believe infidelity took a back seat to money. Just sick! Not to mention that whatever college money was left the poor bastard wasn't even invited to the campus to check out the school. Thirty-year relationship and it came down to, 'When is the check coming.'"

"It takes two to tango Mike. Besides, the money issue is the law, as you well know. You can't skirt around it." Michael became a little agitated as if I attacked him personally. "Don't give me that two to tango crap Vince. If you aren't happy you get out, before you start screwing around. I don't have to tell you what I think she is..."

"Okay Mike, I get the picture...not my fault buddy. I don't make the rules or understand why people do what they do." His mood lightened. "I'm taking another French fry you bastard," he said, sardonically.

"Funny thing is my friend is so good natured. If his divorce came up with you he will just slyly stare at you, wipe his thin dastardly mustache, and say, 'Yep, I'm one of the first

Facebook casualties.'

"Seriously Vince, I'm sure you remember your own divorce. For some of us it is still fresh. Another buddy of mine still cries, and sometimes the loneliness suffocates him. I don't think women truly understand how long it takes for a man to bounce back. And not just married men, long relationships can hurt just as much." He waved his hand to pause. "Well a lot more than they think."

"Not all women have it easy you know."

"I know that once they are done with you, they are done with you."

Where have I heard that before? "Eat something," I said.

"I'm getting some pie and more coffee." Michael ordered a waffle with chocolate ice cream. I was delighted. At least it appeared he would be eating willingly. Yet I knew we were soon going to venture into some serious business. Michael went out for yet another smoke while we waited for dessert. I reflected on this project and its emotional undertaking. I still couldn't believe what we were all going through with this venture of serious guy talk. I almost felt like having a cigarette myself.

"Mmm," he said, filling a fork full of ice cream and waffle.

"I know you lost weight since this whole ordeal," I said.

"Yes, 28 pounds to be exact."

"You still look good," I smiled.

Changing the subject, he announced, "Is there really any more to say? I mean after a while a person gets tired of discussing his problems. Actually, the people who pretend to listen get more exhausted. My family. What I have put them through with my babbling. Selfish. My friends...After a while I didn't even want anyone's opinions...It got to the point where each of them wanted to take the wheel and dictate what I should do.

"I even went to a priest. He was a man of age who no doubt has had many conversations on the subject of divorce. But he didn't preach the sanctity of marriage. Instead he wished me well and assured me I eventually will be okay... I told him with all the struggles and tragedies in the world, I had no right to complain, but he said to me,

'This is your struggle. Your tragedy and you have a right to ask God for his help.'"

"Can you offer a continued conversation?"

"You mean advice of some sort?"

"Sort of..." I asked. "What is a day like for you?"

"Let's see," he said. "I wake up upset and I go to sleep upset. I think of my deep regrets. But I try to move on. I have plenty of family so loneliness is only when I'm alone. I go out two or three times a week, though my body ain't what it used to be."

Knowing his indulgences, I said, "I think you should try to socialize more without getting so annihilated where you can't talk with anyone. Just a suggestion." He gave me a glaring look. Still, I cautioned him on the dangers of self destruction without trying to get a rise out of him.

"What are you looking for now," I asked.

"Well, to tell you the truth, first I'm no misogynist and I'm certainly not the best-looking guy in the world but as a matter of fact, I'm looking for a good looking woman. Try going on these dating sites. You could rifle through a hundred photos and maybe hit one that appeals to you."

"Isn't that selfish?" I said. "Whatever happened to beauty on the inside?"

"Well, like my brother always says, 'it is what it is.'

"Well anyway buddy, switching gears, all I could say is that I believe a man is offered the chance to have three loves of his life. Yet, all those years ago, in my adolescent fantasies, I wanted to meet just one, from the beginning until the end...anyway." He counted on his fingers. "I had one in the 1970's, one in the 80's, and I married in the 90's. I believe I exhausted my three tries."

"There is always a fourth, maybe a soul-mate," I smiled.

"Come on Vin. How old are we? Listen to yourself. You don't need to answer but be honest with yourself. Did you ever really have a soul mate? What the hell is that anyway except some fantasy dreamed up in movies?

"I just want a companion," he said. "No more great loves. Besides at my age who needs the aggravation."

Even as I understood his pain, saw his pain, I pushed anyway. "You can't stop cupid."

"No but you can control stupidity. Going through this crap again with the hope it will begin as a new love is like drinking the proverbial Kool-Aid."

We laughed out loud and a couple seated at a small table behind us definitely heard our small commotion.

Michael went from laugh to frown in an instant.

"If things between two people are so bad, but you know in your heart you love your wife, or husband, and then keep trying, again and again and again. You just might be ending a relationship with true love." *(Why can't you and mom just sit down and have a conversation)*.
He wanted to continue further but he needed a cigarette.

"You're going to smoke in the rain again?"

Then I realized, what's the use, he didn't care anyhow.

"It's just a mist," Michael said. "Besides I'll stand under the awning."

He returned telling me not only were cigarettes his vice but that he had fallen into a world of self-flagellation. I already knew that.

"You mean you hurt yourself in some way?" I asked.

"No, I don't mean the whip with the claws and nails attached, and no I don't mean thoughts of suicide either. I've seen a few of those in my days and they are not pretty. No, my torment is self-pity bordering on self-deprecation." He said this with quick honesty as to not relent. He referred to his admission to me about wild nights of alcohol and pills. "They plainly made me forget for a little while...There was actually a time when I felt like if I went to a doctor and he told me I was terminal I wouldn't have given a shit."

"You don't mean that."

"Hell I don't!" He rolled his finger around his midsection. "Stomach cancer, like my father."

"Mike, I'm going to ask you a serious and potentially painful question. Actually this is a theme or question that will go out there to all of you."

"Okay, so it's not personal," he said, raising an eyebrow.

"No," I smiled. "Anyway, I have to ask you. Through all this unwanted experience, describe to me one of your worst moments."

"Wow," he said. "That's tough since there have been many." He put his hand to his chin, "Give me a moment," he said.

"All the time in the world," I replied. "I know it's a tough one." I've had to ask myself the same question many times. I wanted to remember my own pain before I could ask someone else.

Michael began "I was in my apartment alone one night. It was the first week I had moved in, so the reality was that I was officially alone, officially separated so to speak. It was a weekday, there was nowhere to go, and I didn't feel like bothering anyone with my problems this particular night. I started drinking bourbon. Drinking alone with depression was not a habit of mine but at that moment in my life, it became a crutch for me... I paced and paced this tiny apartment until I was dizzy. I didn't even put the television on. Sort of like when I walked around that strip mall in Florida only there was no fresh air circling around me.

"Over and over I wondered about my mistakes. My resentments, feeling like a third wheel in a house full of women. I don't know I thought a father and a husband deserved more respect. But I also knew it was my fault, always afraid to make a decision they wouldn't like. And by trying to appease them all, I lost everyone's respect.

"And I knew. In one fell swoop I felt as if a basket of old and future memories were taken from me. This is going to sound a little freaky, but I began to sob, uncontrollably. I remember lighting a cigarette to calm down but that first long drag I almost choked and almost dry-heaved. Then out of nowhere I began to scream, almost beastly, AHHHH, AHHHH. I shouted, 'WHY, WHY, WHY. GOD, GOD, WHAT DID I DO?' I shouted out their names, my wife, and my children. I literally felt the tears soak my face. I felt there was no way out of that room and the walls were suffocating me. How's that for melodrama. But it's all true-100 %. I don't have to tell you what the body feels after an experience like that."

"Michael---"

"I'll tell you anyway. You feel like retching. Even if it's dry heaving and your sick to your stomach." I let him pause as he looked down and away. I was hoping he wouldn't break

34

down. I would have felt extremely guilty. He didn't but he went on. "I thought only women did that," he said. "Still, I got through it and many similar nights afterwards. Not good stuff. But I thought maybe that's what I deserved."

"Hating oneself… I don't think you deserved it."

I decided not to venture anymore in the macabre. I explained to him that what he experienced was a familiar loneliness and I tried to assure him that nothing is permanent. I do believe somewhere in his soul Michael is extremely conscious of what he needs to do to move on beginning with enjoying the simple pleasures that he had always found solace in, writing in a journal, reading more books, and seeing more movies. He was also going to actively seek a part time job, if not for the money but to keep him busy.

In the end, with a judges warning, to settle and settle quickly, Michael was rewarded the money he deserved, nothing more, nothing less. If his wife wanted to spend more money in court by spiting him then so be it. It was an attorneys dream.

"I felt dirty going into court," Michael told me. "I was labeled the *Defendant* and I felt like a criminal going through the detectors and all."

However, in an ironic twist, both attorneys in this case suggested a quick end to the matter. They agreed that their clients would just be wasting tons of money in court fees. Michael would joke he never wore his suit so much than during that time.

He continued with his idea of what married souls strive for. He reiterated again that if there were any speck of love left, keep trying to reconcile your differences, and then try some more "Don't let the silence get out of hand," he said. His expression when mentioning his children always conveyed the pain of a man who knows he would never get those lost days back, where the family nucleus created a world of its own memories. The trips to Hershey Park, *(Come on Dad, Mom's going on with us, the roller coaster won't make you sick)*, the purchase of their first home, the births, the first pool for the family to swim in, school events, looking at colleges and on and on... "I can't even look at old photos without feeling sad. Does she remember those things?" A hurt man can sound quite poetic and I told him as much, especially when remembering the eternal order of his life.

"Maybe," he said. "How's this for poetry," he continued.

"My wife very straightforwardly, almost wantonly, told me to be careful what I wished for. She told me to get over it. She was tired of me and able to shut me out without reservation... Does that make the memories a lie?

"To paraphrase Dante: 'You shall be banished, leaving everything you love.'"

"Almost sinister," I answered, in regards to his wife's biting statement. But you know as well as I do those memories, though not exactly truth, are not lies."

"You know what really hurts at the end? I remember when we first started dating. I was up front about my neurosis. I always was possessed with some form of sadness I could never shake...She promised to see me through it all. She told me as she hugged me, that she wished she could take away any troubles I felt...But I guess there were promises I made as well. Still, there was never anything so serious that a little faith couldn't have cured."

"How so," I answered.

"The big three. He held up his three middle fingers.

"There was never any violence. No embarrassing or abusive drunken episodes." He left his middle finger up as a pun. "And no infidelity. She put up with my moods and I

36

put up with her coldness. It worked for a very long time."

I was pleased that Michael had publicly opened up to me as much as he did. I believed it was a road to recovery letting out the stuffing that had lain dormant for many months. I know it hurt him deeply to be another statistic, one of more than 50% who don't make it. He wasn't in the percentile of men who are genuinely glad to be divorced.

"I know this conflicts with some of my ideas but I guess if we can't get the help to work it out," he stated. "Then why would anyone want to go back into the frozen tundra? I have been told that a million times as to why I would return to the same old crap...the discomfort in which former lovers feel. Always wondering if it will really work out...You know how many family disputes I witnessed and said to myself at those times, when screaming vicious people were attacking each other. I said, holy shit that could never be me...What a laugh!

"For argument sake, even if there was a renewed love between me and my wife it would never work for one simple fact...Any argument, whether I start it or she does is going to be construed as here we go again. There will always then be regrets that we wasted our time, again. It's just unavoidable. All these proclamations of longing and regret I now make. It's just human nature to forget once you're complacent again."

"I hear you. It would be quite difficult to resume a relationship with that kind of pressure." I certainly couldn't argue with that one. I felt exactly the same after my marriage ended. I went on. "Is there anything that is decisively better in your life now?" I asked him with a good humored chuckle.
"Yeah, I could nap when I want, pick my nose, watch whatever on TV, make a mess, the proverbial scratch my balls right there on the couch. I could choose my own

clothes, grow my hair, grow a beard and take no direct and ridiculous orders!" Together we laughed heartily.

"You know my friend," I said. "It certainly is good to remember the old wonderful trips down memory lane. But maybe you could try to understand why you are here in this place to begin with. I know it's the miscommunication, the coldness, your moods, but is there anything that you could roll off your tongue right now that would immediately doubt her love for you-hypothetically even?"

"Whenever I got a new car she didn't want to go for a ride in it-when I wrote something she didn't care to read it-- when my dad passed I didn't get that tight warm I'm sorry hug--and when we reunited during our last split and we were lying in bed I turned to her and said, 'God I love you'- - her response---nothing---absolutely nothing! --How's that for rolling off my tongue?"

Wow, I thought. Here was the honesty right here in a bottle. I was blown away. Even as he was protected by anonymity would he even want me to print this? It was raw, pure nakedness.

I watched as his lips tightened to a frown. I needed to ask him one more serious question. "Michael if you had the chance, is there anything you would say to your wife?" I also asked him why he wore his wedding band on his right finger.

He looked at the ring, tugged on it gently and he smiled. "Of course it holds on to a piece of life I regret leaving for the greener grass. Actually the real wedding band was gold with our names inscribed. I left that for her in our safe, along with a beautiful Swiss watch she had bought for me early in our marriage. Who knows maybe she sold them. I just couldn't. Anyway there is a pint of humor in the silver band I wear now. When women ask me why I still wear it-- and they do notice it--I tell them it reminds me never to put one on my left finger again."

He appeared as if he were recollecting an image. He was.

"You know on the day we married the limo was so hot we thought it was because of the August heat." He released a little laugh. "It was the air conditioner. The limo driver had the gauge set to hot." He told me of a now funny incident that happened on his honeymoon, though I'm sure it wasn't funny then. He had gone out knee boarding because he couldn't water ski. His wife was good at skiing and he recollected her gracefully staying up in the water. So his board flipped over and he felt like he was drowning. He panicked and couldn't turn himself upright. "My wife didn't know but I wondered what if I drowned that day? I'd be remembered for my youth not some white haired 50 something."

"Terrible way to die," I responded. We laughed.

Recollection is not a bad thing unless you obsess over it. I also loved his analogy of the explaining his ring wearing to women. I confessed to him that upon my own divorce I would automatically focus in on a woman's wedding ring finger to see if she was attached.

Michael went on to explain what he deemed a guilty sadness. He told me that he knew for sure one of his wife's dreams was to be married 50 years. Celebrate the golden years together. "As for me," he said. "Never mattered much, not even a silver anniversary. But I wanted to give her her due. People I guess still believe in the American white picket fence crap.

"As far as what I would say...She once said to me, post separation, 'You can't even look me in the eye.' I would tell her she was right but it wasn't because of anything she did--I would say to her, 'because you remind me of my own shortcomings. My inability to sustain any kind of relationship for long periods of time…'I would explain that

I had tried everything from counseling to medication, to God, even meditation. Nothing seemed to work.

"I even went as far--after I read something--it was about a stone --that if you rubbed this stone each morning you could find some semblance of peace. Ironically in a playful mood one night she tossed this stone she grabbed from a fixture dish in our home. For whatever reason I had placed it my desk drawer then found it when I moved out...I carried it around in my pocket for a long time.

"Anyway, I would admit my faults, and admit I said things because I thought she didn't understand me and she deserved to hurt just as much as me. Not to mention my threats of divorce instead of the maturity to be able to discuss what the hell we had just argued about. To pull my emotions off the floor and deal with the moment...

"And my jovial demeanor when I told her I had found an apartment and got myself a post office box to retrieve my mail...That wasn't very nice of me.

"Oh, let me roll one more thing off my tongue. She never even asked me for a matter of fact answer about the whole unable to look at her thing. Like she wasn't even curious." Michael took a breath out and I hoped I wasn't increasing his anxiety. He assured me I wasn't and he was glad for the question.

"I would want to explain to her that I know things were supposed to end amicably but as humans go there will always be an array of feelings and emotions that naturally take over and prevent a cartoon or misguided movie image of amicability...And to exasperate the finish there was no need for her to turn me off like a light bulb and admit as much by saying she had just had enough of me..."

Michael swallowed and gasped...

"Please---"

"No," he cut in. "I want to say my piece." He continued never looking me in the eye; instead staring down at was left of his soggy waffle. "I would ask her why she treated me like a total stranger. Why she kept using the excuse that I was argumentative when I was argumentative for twenty years. I'm Italian. Argumentative is a way of life in my family. *(Dad! Stop yelling at Mom!)*. I would reiterate over and over about the big three we discussed, that those things never happened and that is why in post-divorce she should have shown some concern for me...I would explain my reason for changing the divorce agreement a million times. Not for money but to prolong the process hoping we could one day speak about what happened? I was searching for that last bit of hope. But that day never came...Any credibility I had left with her went out the window during the settlement phase and the dreaded and unexpected court battle. I could say I promise this or I assure you of that and it would mean absolutely nothing...Those awkward moments in court were like a betrayal as deeply wounding as infidelity."

For a sec I thought of my own divorce court days. All the couples filling the courtroom, not so much as looking at each other, even as they voiced their complaints. 'Welcome to divorce court,' I once heard an attorney joke. I wanted to grab him by the collar and scream, 'Do you think this is a fucking joke?!'

To me, attorneys are vipers who search out clients like dogs sniffing the piss scent off a fire hydrant. Standing around that court made my jaw clench so tight I thought my teeth would break.

"Believe me, and again I'm not wife bashing but she is a master at freezing someone out. Her coldness can become permanent. She could go weeks without talking for something you would forget the argument was about in the first place. Well, that is her way and this is my interpretation of the story...I should hate her. But it's like my grandmother used to say, 'Rapporto amore odio,' Love-hate relationship."

I admired Michael. Once again, the look of sadness on his face was heart wrenching. Especially when he told of his romantically scripted fantasy, his last long love letter. His lingering wish after a long life was to die in her arms, or at least her holding his hand tenderly on his deathbed. I once felt the same way though I don't remember it as being as intense. Who knows, maybe by my ending nuptials I had nothing left to care about. Man, one could learn a lot by hanging out with guys sailing in sinking boats.

"Again, it will feel like I am venting for a long time to come. She's like a ghost to me now, an antiquity. I don't even know who she is...During one of the very few conversations we had I said to her that not once did I ever say I didn't love you. In response I got nothing-nada. When my brother implied to her that she might have pushed me out he got the same reply-nada. And her nothing replies always told of her honest nature. Being cold never made her a liar. If she doesn't tell you an answer you're getting it. Anyway, it's amazing how love can turn on a dime-just like that," he said snapping his fingers. "Just six months ago we were barbecuing burgers, or should I say she was. She was better at it than I. The kids were in the pool splashing around. *(Check out this dive)*. You feel the distance but never really believe... Do you know how many rivers of tears I cried my friend?"

"I do," I answered.

"No, I literally cried and cried and screamed and yelled when I was alone. I was like a lunatic. If I ever saw someone act the way I was, I would truly think they were in need of a straightjacket. It was like being at a scream park."

(Dad, I ain't going in that haunted house!)

"I admire your courage Mike, and am so sorry for what you have been through." I said sincerely. "I just want to ask one thing. Can it be possible that just maybe…"

He rolled his eyes. "Here comes your both sides thing, right?" Mike said.

"All I'm saying is there is a remote chance that your wife has suffered as much as you have."

"I don't--"

Now I cut him off. "Hear me. Maybe her loss is as great as yours, maybe she grieves the loss of a future she had planned with you. Maybe distance is her only way of coping.
If she was sub-human the kids would have felt it, they would have said something to you."

"True."

"And I have no doubt. Hey, you did say they were an animal of a different color…Didn't you tell me, that in the days leading up to your departure you noticed she would lay in bed more than she should have been-don't answer my friend. She could have been very depressed!"

I continued before Michael could jump in and maybe twist the WHOLE story to his, victim like advantage.
"You did admit you zinged her with the apartment and Post Office thing."

"Yeah and she zinged me pretty good with all the guilt you could lay on this planet. Telling me that if I took, which by the way I wasn't taking, it belonged to me, but if I took equal property I was a lousy selfish bastard! It was I who had to earn, not only her respect, but the kids' as well. Their word was more believable to her than mine. Jesus why couldn't we be on the same page as parents? What the fuck!"

"I didn't want you to get upset pal---"

"Why the hell not? Isn't it the point of this exercise? Isn't this supposed to be my microscopic tale of woe? Shouldn't I say how utterly pissed off I was to believe she meant one word. To wrap my head around the idea that now she would twist the truth. Telling me the money should stay with her because she didn't know what her future would hold. Not to mention she announced she did not trust me with any money. Then I find out the week I was supposed to sign the damn papers she got a huge promotion and raise---they don't tell you that you're getting promoted overnight. She knew."

"I got it Mike. You deserve to vent. But can I just say who really knows? I mean what did you expect, to be coddled?"

"No! I didn't. I've been down that road before. I froze out relationships so I wouldn't be perceived as the guilty party. I know if you no longer love someone it's hard to coddle, as you say. Still, a little honesty would have been nice. Tell me you don't love me. Make that clear before any amicability, this way I wouldn't construe friendship in any romantic way. But again this is my grieving, my interpretation, and I am not looking for answers about why love had died.

"I never said I was the nicest guy. I'll concede that-- maybe. I've woken up on the wrong side of the bed many times. I could certainly be a hypocrite in family matters. You know, my family was right in situations that would have made her family seem wrong. But I'll tell you; I wasn't the worst guy either. Again, I have admitted my share...When she would come home exhausted from a long day of work and you could just see the weariness on her face, I should have been more helpful, I shouldn't have complained to her how hard my day was trying to raise three kids.

"Yes I am sure my moods scared her at times. Actually, I'm

certain of it. Sometimes I live in a dark space. No excuses, it's how I'm wired. I know it can't be easy living with the idea that a man might just disappear one day, or wake up sad for no reason. She knew I suffered bouts of melancholia. If the shoe were on the other foot, I would honestly say I don't know if I could handle that. But right now that's neither here or there.

"I was the only one on the planet that didn't realize she just didn't give a shit about me anymore. Still she wanted all the control, even after the split. In the end I realize that if I don't take back my life no one else can do it for me. Should I have sacrificed more? I already lost one apartment because I couldn't afford it. I'm living way below her, but that's fine, she's with the kids but still nobody gives a shit. As my kids get further apart from my family and me she's no help. She should remind them to call, or at least answer a fucking text! I'm afraid to say anything to them even when they are wrong, for fear they won't talk to me."

Michael ran his nervous hand through his hair and exhaled. I didn't say a word.

"How long should I walk around with knots in my stomach?" he continued "These games men and woman play. It's like war. Who's going to win, who is smarter and has the upper hand. Who will get the last word? And for what? Just to hurt each other? It's all bullshit!"

War. I thought about his defense offense comment. So true.

"I'm rambling but I want to say thank you my friend." He grabbed my hand with both of his. He had gone on a roller

coaster of thoughts all over the place. He was clearly spent of emotion. "Vince," he continued. "There is a poetic line from this song that is so profound. God knows I have listened to enough suicide songs to last me a lifetime." We laughed.

45

"Sinatra's version of the song is my favorite and I can repeat this like a mantra- 'its love's illusions I recall, but I really don't know love at all, at all.' And I don't."

We parted and it was bittersweet. I knew I had found a good friend, someone I actually had more in common with than I had thought. Yet I was sad. He voluntarily retold what I knew was as traumatic as death for him. The feeling of loss might shrink but he would never forget; for it would never go away. His shortcomings together with his wife's inability to live with his doubt, and any more patience, solidified a decision that only they two know if they would regret it. I never met his wife, but from his side of the story it seemed she was treating Michael like a vassal, that she was superior to him in all decisions.

In the end he baited her and she bit. Or as I couldn't make him want to hear, that it just happens, that people grow apart.

Unlike those who have advised Mike to just get over it, I tread lightly and encourage him to take baby steps if need be. Only Michael can decide when and where to move on. For too long he has been in a kind of suspended disbelief. For too long he has wallowed in self-pity. He now has that opportunity to embrace some longings that maybe were meant to be. Retreat, maybe come to understand life more, walk along the water or into the trees. Take a trip to Europe and most importantly real quality time with his kids. I know he doesn't mind me saying that he has some work, especially in those dark moments where he believes whatever gets him through the night.

I cannot judge anyone, let alone a man who has been so forthright. I pity his lost first year of holidays, birthdays, and even his anniversary, a day when he had sat in the parking lot of the town park for hours listening to music and remembering the times he spent with his family and their friends and the kid's softball games. *(Was that a hit? Was it?)* It was extremely tough for him, for any parent to decipher the feelings of loss and rejection. To be able to know the difference when your kids didn't call or forgot to call. *(What's the big deal dad?)*

Yet he told me, "I had to read them the riot act so to speak...had to tell them that they couldn't call me just to get them fast food and then drop them off. I told them it just wasn't fair. I needed our alone time." Michael trailed off... "Talk about what was going on in their lives."

I had no doubt that Michael would hurt for some time even if he began to have some periods of happiness.

When we said our goodbyes in the parking lot he surprised me. We hugged each other and suddenly he began to cry. I didn't expect it. He lingered on my shoulder until he could somewhat compose himself. I felt in that moment helpless almost uncomfortable as if Michael were a brother that I could not give any relief to. This whole ordeal was kind of banging my head around a little too.

My parting words were," I believe you will be free of this seemingly unending nightmare." Though, who really could predict when? I didn't mention to him that I truly felt bad for his wife as well. Divorce just couldn't be sitting well with her either.

I consider Michael one of a handful of people I really enjoy having long conversations with, when we get the chance. As life goes through spurts of relationships, I don't see Mike as much as I thought I would. We somehow get drawn back to into our circle of friends and family we are comfortable with. We all wanted to embark on a project together that would somehow make sense to us. It started as an idea from my friend Jayson and we just all rolled with it. Michael is now officially divorced. He confessed to me that it really hit home after the ink was dry on the divorce. And after he picked up his kids after school, he walked into the house and immediately noticed with a faint heart, all the pictures that he and his wife were together in, were now down, off the walls and off the mantles. The photos that had him, his wife and children on sunny vacations were especially difficult to see absent. For an entire year there were a few wedding photos and family pictures still adorning the common places in the home.

He had come to realize they were kept there for the kids, that his ex-wife was not torturing him, reminding him of his loss every time he walked in, but she was protecting the children with the knowledge that until they were divorced and ready for everyone to move on, she kept those photographs up for them. Still it hurt. He feels bad about going into the house where memories are strong. Even greeting the family dog was painful. He explained it to the kids that for now he just didn't feel right hanging around the home and he thinks they understood, though they had that confused look on their faces. He lied and told them it had nothing to do with their mother.

Michael admitted that on occasion he still, out of habit, referred to his ex-wife as his wife and that in many instances he would talk to be people he didn't know much and speak as if he still lived at home. "Crazy," he said. "But I don't feel like discussing my divorce with just anyone."

I did explain to him that part of the process of moving on was to not cross up his life with any lies.

His pain lingers but is less, his relationship with his children holding strong, yet cautious. He really tries not to excite disappointment. *(Can't make it today Dad. Forgot I had plans).* His anger has made way for disappointment. He relies on his own opinions now after many months of well meant but conflicting advice. He prefers not to discuss his ex-wife or their relationship only saying that it's cordial. I had high hopes that they would be truthfully forgiving to one another, especially knowing that some of his final words to her were stinging. He told her upon the divorce, 'I don't even want to breathe the same air as you.' But I know the man, and usually when Michael said something hurtful, he was hurting himself.

To put it somewhat Shakespearian, I believe Michael is a romantically tragic figure. A person who possesses a chameleon-like personality; a regular guy who fits in with whatever circle he's chosen to hang with on any given day. He is fallible just like any other human being. But deep in his heart he stands on that artist's ledge.

He is a person with true sentiment who has harbored great thoughts of art and of romance. In classic form, love is supposed to be synonymous with pain. Some ideas are too fictitious to presume to be real. He might even not like me mentioning these types of characteristics but I wondered reluctantly if he would wander aimlessly through his life trying to decipher some kind of meaning to any relationship that he ever had. If he would forever try to piece together what the meaning of all his romantic relationships were truly about. Why if he wasn't destined to remain with one permanently. He was that profound. But in some fool drudgery way I think the angst prevented him from truly hating himself. The angst was artistic, a writer or an actor's angst.

Eventually Michael was thrown another curve. I don't know but somehow I thought it would be some kind of closure even as I knew this man would feel it deep into the pit of his stomach. He'd learned that his ex-wife was in a serious relationship with a new lover. To Michael, no matter how anyone would try to convince him of his opinion, he was convinced that his suspicions of another person surfacing after his divorce had come to pass.

When he first learned of his ex-wife's new partner he informed his children that he didn't care to know their mother's boyfriends name, didn't care where they met or why. He just wanted to know immediately if the new guy ever treated his kids disrespectfully.

Last time I did see Michael, I was in a nightclub in East Meadow. A place where the middle-aged could still congregate. Strangely the decor of the place and lingering odor from the carpets made you actually feel you were back in the 80's.

I was with some buddies and was delighted when I spotted my old friend on the other side of the dance floor. He was free-style dancing semi grinding with a blond cutie and he seemed delighted. He came over and we were happy to see each other.

"You think that's the same disco ball from years ago?" I said, pointing at the small-glassed strobe above the center of the dance floor.

He laughed. "Does it even turn? Or is that the lights making all that phony magic?"

"Who cares?" I answered.

I asked him if he was Okay. Though he seemed cozy with this new woman he still confessed. "Yes, I'm fine," he replied. "I must admit after I found out about the ex's boyfriend I had to hit the Xanax bottle again. Strangely at that moment the break-up seemed fresh again. Anyway, just when I had weaned myself off."

For a second I wondered if the Xanax produced the symptoms of his constant smoking. I knew it didn't mix well with drinking.

"Just take it easy," I preached. Looking towards the blonde who was now dancing with a girlfriend of hers I said, "I see your succeeding with the good-looking girl remedy."

He smiled and answered, "I was actually hoping for a brunette; the complete opposite of my ex. But you take what you could get out here."

I asked him of his nights of carousing. "I have fun once in a while," he told me, his smile full. "But don't get too excited. There are plenty of nights out here full of disappointment, rejection and that feeling of loneliness. I walk around feeling dead on occasion."

"Had to throw the negative in," I said.

"Sure, why not. Fact is, most people out in this scene have been beat up and lived through many of their own tears. They don't even know themselves what they are looking for... everyone recollects their lives with unconscious editing...

"You give your phone number out. You collect a bunch of numbers. The ones you are interested in don't call back and vice versa. It's mass hysteria...Many of these people you only see every other week because of who has the children that particular weekend." He flipped his thumb in the direction of his date. "She's a victim. Her ex-husband still haunts her and now uses the kids. She was sick one weekend and the bastard told the children she faked it so she wouldn't have to take them out and spend money on them. Then he told them their mother uses the child support to party. What a ---"

"See my friend," I cut in. "It unfortunately works both ways with cruelty."

"I guess. But this woman deserves to go out and have fun. Hey why don't you come out more often?" he said.

"Are you kiddin', after what you just told me." I laughed.

"It ain't all bad," he said. Look around. I'm back to my pre-marital days." He laughed with tight lips. "I live in someone's basement apartment. Well you know I was never one for house planting and mowing the lawn. I've come to appreciate spaghetti and peanut butter and jelly sandwiches."

I only commented on his going out. "I should meet you more often," I replied. "Maybe I will learn a thing or two."

Michael put both his hands on my shoulders and looked at me through glassy eyes. He was dressed with style, a blue button down shirt to contrast his eyes, but he was lit up. I preferred to see him clear eyed and philosophical. He also had to speak a little louder, over the thumping music, not to mention he was fifteen percent deaf in both ears. His voice was again raspy, almost like he was filled with phlegm and needed to spit. I am sure after a night of drinking he had probably smoked a whole pack just in the last few hours.

"You know what a movie freak I am," he said. "There are two movies made about love that left the viewer seriously dangling."

I was perplexed. What analogy was Mike going' to make about his own life?

"And?" I asked.

"I didn't like the endings because as a movie fan I want it one way or another. I want the happy or the sad, but I want an answer...sort of like I would in life."

"Where are we going with this buddy?"

"I don't like a story without an ending but now I have to buy into some of the critics who say there just ain't any definitive answer. The purpose of no resolution is goddamned haunting."

I let him go on because I was certain he wanted to make this point with me, the guy who delved into his soul pulling out his honest answers. Besides his eyes were watery from booze and smoke and he wasn't going to let it go until he finished his point.

"...Both movies ended with hands." Michael turned his palms up at me. "The coupling of the hands was to convey to the audience if the couple are staying together or at least still in love. It is almost spiritual like in a mural, hands reaching out."

"So, you still have no closure I assume? Or do you?" I couldn't figure it out.

He didn't answer just went on about the images of some movies.

"And I get that it might not ever be. I get the films were trying to get us the viewer to figure it out."

I didn't want to stop him but he was not one hundred percent making sense to me.

He heaved out a sigh and I could smell both the smoke and the drink. "No, nothing as dramatic as me and my ex our hands touching on screen, but I left a reminder behind."

"You got me curious buddy, what?"

"After the divorce I sent her flowers."

"Oh no Mike, please tell me--"

"No, no. I didn't leave a note or profess my love. I just sent a huge bouquet to her office, no roses... You know why no roses? My ex-wife has to be one of the few women in the world who does not like roses. I always brought her bouquets with no roses."

"Michael."

"Don't you see? Only I know she don't care for roses, so when she got them I thought even if she wondered who sent them, another guy, whoever, why wasn't there any roses. Would she always wonder if it were me?"

"Your sense for the dramatic doesn't surprise me."

Although I had to believe he would know she would eventually at least skim through this book.

"Like the films, I left us to wonder, get it."

"I got it buddy, so long as you do."

"I do pal, I do." He leaned in hugged me and kissed me Italian style on both cheeks. Leaving, walking back to his group of friends as I did mine, he winked at me, "My pockets don't weigh me down anymore." I didn't get it at first, and then I remembered the stone. He doesn't carry it anymore!

Chris

"God deals you a hand, you play it"
                                                                ~Chris L.

I asked Chris if I could meet him at the Woodbury-Syosset ball fields where he was photographing a charity softball game between police officers from both Nassau and Suffolk counties. You could not have asked for a better day to have a ballgame, which honored our fallen local heroes and their family members. The player's uniforms were adorned with bright colors. The reds and the royal blues would "pop" right off the print, which is a great trait to capture in a photograph. The donations from the afternoon's event were to be distributed amongst various children's organizations throughout Long Island including agencies, which took care of the children of police officers killed in the line of duty. Chris was an avid shutterbug in his hometown where he shot many of his kids sporting events as well as events (fairs and such) for the local papers; where many of his photos could regularly be seen. Some were even exhibited inside Town Hall and on occasion, in the local branch of the public library.

The funny thing about Chris is that he is this really gentle guy, and considering his size, he could be disarmingly kind.

He hovers around 6'1 and weighs close to 275 pounds. Don't get me wrong. If you are on the opposite side of his friendship, and provoke him in anyway, he could knock you over with one swipe of his bear like paws. Here's a guy that shouldn't let his glasses fool you, he is no dweeb. I know one story to be more than fable pertaining to his switch from Gentle Ben to grizzly.

It goes that while at work one day, during a domestic dispute, Chris was faced down by someone even bigger than he. The imbecile was slobbering drunk and didn't take too kindly to Chris being in his house at that particular moment. *"This is my house and I don't want you or any of you police in it!"* Chris attempted to reason with the disorderly husband. He didn't want anything getting out of control in front of the guy's family. The man had young kids who were terrified, crying and cowed down on the couch, huddled next to their beleaguered mother like baby cubs. So Chris coerced the guy to walk outside with him, where the drunk continued his belligerent and obnoxious behavior. He stupidly raised a hand toward Chris. Chris instinctively swiped the guy's forearm aside, and then swung a backhand full of knuckles into the guy's cheek with a force that could have been heard around the corner. This big hunk of nonsense went down like a rock. "Now are you going to listen? Or do I have to lock you up?" he said. The contentious but defeated drunk was then all ears.

So now, today, after all the smiles, handshakes, high fives, and the wonderful action shots, the hellos, the thanks, and goodbyes, I gestured toward a nearby picnic table. Certainly not like the structure that my office, and pay scale afforded me, but comfortable enough to ask the big man some deeply personal questions.

Chris is two years separated from a marriage that lasted twenty years and produced three children whom Chris refers to as 'The Boys.' The smile on big Chris' face when he mentions his kids is electric. The man simply adores his children. Still he tries to remain humble and careful not to brag at how exceptional they are in all their chosen sports.

Not to mention their respect and good manners to all persons they encounter; manners taught by both parents.

As if we rehearsed it, Chris went to his car to stow away his camera bags and I walked to mine and retrieved a bag from my front seat consisting of a couple of bags of chips and a few bottles of water. I suggested the empty picnic table close to the park clubhouse. He nervously laughed a little when I took out my notebook and pen.

Even as it was late afternoon the day was a really spectacular spring unfolding. It was serene as no one occupied the adjoining tables and the sounds that filled the park were barely audible. Chris smiled and clasped those big hands together. "OK, let's do this buddy," he said.

"So," I began. "Two years out of your marriage. But you're not officially divorced yet?"

"No, the wheels of the courts turn very slowly and very expensively."

I had to laugh along because stereotypes are usually never far from the truth and the divorce lawyers and courts unfortunately almost always live up to their reputation. It's all about the money for them.

"Can you humor me and say something that will put a smile on your face?"

"Why is it that we have to renew our driver's license, our fishing license, our hunting license, our broker's license; every other type of license but our marriage license?" Chris joked.

"No, seriously", I asked. "Do you have any kind of relationship with your ex?"

"Yes," he said boldly. "She still hates me."

I couldn't help but chuckle.

"What caused all this Chris?"

"Bottom line, I wasn't happy. I know its sound oversimplified with just three little words, but so do the words 'I Love You.' I mean, there is so much behind both sets of words, so much good and so much bad, but in my case, it really came down to that fact; for some reason, I wasn't happy. I started to feel as if, I don't know, I started to feel as if I really didn't matter. I didn't matter to anyone anymore. I really can't put a finger on exactly when I started to feel that way, but somewhere along the way, I really felt like I no longer mattered."

"How could you feel that way?" I asked.

"I don't know…I guess it was something that was brewing in me for a really long time. I worked a lot. Always did some side job so everyone had enough money to do what they had to do. We had the proverbial "money envelope" in the kitchen cabinet. I would always either work a security gig or do something to put a few extra dollars in that envelope. The extra cash was always there. It was like the "Fun Fund" for going into the city to see plays, trips to out of state amusement parks, or the travel sports and all the expenses that came with that. There was always some cash on hand to go anywhere on a whim or do anything that we wanted to do.

"It just seemed like I was the one who made sure it was all taken care of. I remember, my famous line was always, 'I'll take care of it.' And I did, I always did. I mean no one ever went without. Ya' know, my wife was always my kid's best friend. She did so much with them. Played on the floor with them, took them to theme parks where she would ride the biggest of roller coasters and they would all scream and have a great time and so much fun.

"She was like an adult who always was a kid at heart. We used to jokingly say that she refused to grow up; she just paid adult prices at movie theaters. The boys, they loved that shit! You could see it in their eyes; they loved having a parent who could be fun on their level. Can you understand that? I was like a fucking old man to my kids and she was so much fun."

"Yes, I get that."

"You know what, in hindsight, and I'm being completely honest with you, I guess I started to become jealous of that. She was like their best friend, all the time. She had such a great relationship with them because of that. I guess that just got to me after a while, I don't know maybe I handled it wrong too. I would internalize everything; I never talked about what was bothering me. I did that with everything that bothered me. I still do that. It does nothing but build up a lot of pressure; a lot of pressure that has no choice but to explode one day. She told me later that they would always have to try to guess my mood when I walked into the door. She said that the boys were afraid to say anything to me. I became very short with all of them. I was always miserable. I couldn't believe they were actually afraid of me! To this day, that is something that I have a hard time understanding. How can your own children be afraid of their father? It's not like I was abusive to them. She corrected me constantly; saying I was emotionally abusive. She told me that was when they started to see changes in me. You know what eventually happened? It made them even closer to their mother. Just what I needed, for them to be even closer to their mother! I was dying inside to try to feel accepted, as "one of them," and all it did was end up bringing them closer to her! What a kick in the ass that was."

"So is that why you resented that relationship?" I inquired. "I don't know; I was always 'game on.' Never had fun, I was always too fucking serious I guess... I shouldn't have been. I mean everyone was happy, right? She was happy, the boys were happy, and all the bills got paid. They went wherever they set sail to go, I always just made sure it always happened for everyone…"

"Everyone but you?"

"Yeah, everyone but me…"

Chris became introspective and awkwardly silent. He looked away, then looked up briefly and then looked back down. I could tell that he had just uncovered a whole Pandora's Box of hidden or more precisely, introverted emotions.

He was now on a roll. He was thinking faster than he could talk. It was hard to jot it all down. Then, as if feeling humiliated he appeared to be crumbling.

"Do you want to stop Chris?" I sheepishly asked.
He kept his head down for a moment, glanced weakly upwards at me, smiled through his pain and wiped away a fresh tear. I was watching this giant of a man try to regroup; thoughts filling his mind like water through a broken hull. "No, no, I'm alright. I just need to um, absorb it all for a minute."

"Take your time, do what you need to do." I assured him. *"I started to stop loving her,"* he stated, truthfully. These words came out of his mouth so definitively, so endearing; like he was so sure of the depth their meaning.

It was important that I wrote it exactly the way that he said it. As a writer, I originally found the phrase grammatically awkward. But I soon realized that I had just heard a profound testimony of his true feelings towards his wife.

"I had strayed and by forces that were out of my control, I got exposed…I told my wife afterwards that long before that; I thought the love was gone. I admitted to myself that I was probably living a lie. Like I said earlier, I wasn't happy."

"Was it meaningful? The affair...Did you fall in love?"

"I don't even know what love is. Honestly, I really don't know what is. I could say one thing for sure, and I know that this may sound so fucking weird, but I think that for the first time in my life, I fell in love with myself. That new relationship afforded me that feeling. Maybe it was filling a huge void in my life, I don't know. It felt good to feel appreciated; to feel like you finally *mattered* to someone; like I actually meant something to someone. I've got be honest with you, that felt good, it really did."

He kind of gave me a half-hearted smile when he said that. It was almost as if he was feeling guilty for promoting himself, for putting himself out there. His posture dictated a sense of being very uncomfortable, as if wearing a shirt that didn't quite fit.

"Do you live with the new woman?" I asked.

"Oh no, no, no! But one thing I did know, I had to leave my house. I had caused so much hurt to those that were closest to me that it was the only thing that I could do. It seemed like it had to be done out of respect to my wife and to my children. I knew that I had to go."

"Do you still see her, the other woman that you had the relationship with?"

"Actually, we really don't see each other much anymore. It didn't become what I had hoped it would become."

"I see."

"She harbors a lot of resentment towards me. She also went through a lot with me and now, I don't know, maybe it's not what she thought it would be either. I don't know, I just know that she is not happy where she is right now, she's not happy at all."

"Once the truth came out, how did you justify what you

had done?"

"Well, I made no excuses. I didn't try to deny anything like I said, I was honest about my feelings; I really didn't have any other choice. It's like when they say that a cop will never ask you a question that he doesn't already know the answer to."

As Chris sat reflectively, absorbing his prior admissions, I made a bee-line to the concession stand by the pool area to grab us a couple of sodas as the salty chips seemed to go better with Coke than with water. Chris made me laugh as he yelled to me, "Get me a diet Coke instead of a regular Coke."

Really, I thought. How could a big guy like him with an appetite like a bear be asking for a diet soda? Just get the guy whatever he wants. He's twice your size for Christ's sake. I laughed to myself.

I returned and Chris was tweaking at the crown of his scalp, a habit he had developed long ago. Everyone has their thing I thought. I interrupted him by handing him his diet Coke and we simultaneously popped the straws from their wrappers. I found it to be funny, the both of us unwrapping our straws each in a different fashion; Chris hitting it on the table until the straw broke loose through the top. I chose to gently using two hands; almost peeling the wrapper off as if it was a banana. Two distinct techniques to achieve the same goal; such is life I guess.

Chris needed to finish a thought and said, "I knew it was something that she would never be able to forgive me for. Her convictions regarding the sacrament of marriage were just too strong. She would have to let me go."

I bypassed into the next subject. "How are you getting by without the comfort of your home and your kids?"

"It's so hard. Harder than I ever thought it could be. I

miss everything about my house. I miss falling asleep on the couch, I miss my kids telling me "Get up dad," whenever I would ask them to show me how to 'copy and paste' something as I sat in front of the computer. I miss the notes that they used to leave me on the kitchen counter after coming home from a 4x12, I miss cutting my lawn, weed whacking the sidewalk edges until they looked like Citi Field, washing my car and doing my own oil changes in my own driveway, watching my kids play in the backyard with all their friends, driving them to and from everywhere their busy schedules dictated where they were to be, and taking a full day to clean out the garage (again). Strangers would pass by, stop and ask if we were having a garage sale! That was always funny whenever that happened. What I miss is all the little stuff that wove the fabric of my home life. It sucks actually, it really sucks now.

"I worked hard for everything in that house; the furniture, the cars, the decorating, *everything*. I would make a few extra mortgage payments each year from the overtime checks. They say a man's home is his castle. My kingdom has fallen around me and I have only myself to blame. That was just the answer to the first part of your question. I never fought for the house. It's my children's home.

"This is what they know, where they have grown up. It's their neighborhood. They can walk to their friend's houses and sit outside on the curb. They always knew what day and time the Mr. Softie truck would arrive on the block. They can ride their bikes in the middle of the street and wave to whichever neighbor drives past them. They dogwatch and housesit when other neighbors go away on vacation. It's rightfully theirs; they deserve to stay there.

"I hear about these guys who force their wife to sell the house just to prove a point. Aren't their children suffering enough without having to move from their neighborhood to appease a war of wits? C'mon already! Guys can be such fucking assholes; or maybe I'm just the fool. But I don't think so. There is enough conflict in their lives because of my choices, so why add to the collateral damage."

Chris paused for a moment. I could tell by the look in his eyes that these thoughts were starting to rekindle the embers of some very strong emotions. "It's really a confusing time for them. You can hear that in their silence. You can see that in their faces. They see their mother cry and they don't see me there.

"I really would not want to be going through what they are going through right now. I'm sure that they are confused, angry, alone, and sometimes a bit lost. I can't imagine what goes through their young minds. "The Boys," nah, they don't treat me the same. I guess because things aren't the same. Each of them being individuals with their own thoughts, emotions and opinions as to what went wrong in their parents' relationship. They hold dear, their own beliefs and that needs to be respected. It's as if each of them represents an individual canvas, and they each have a different way of painting their own picture.

"I must put the time in with them. Stay the course. Slowly, only at *their* pace, not mine. I'm not exactly an expert, but I do believe that that is the only way to do it. Their age isn't even the major issue, you have to accept their feelings as gospel and work within each of them; individually. I wish sometimes that they would sit down and talk to me. Just take the time to tell me what is on their minds about what happened then and what they think now. They have never really asked me. I am torn between the fact that either they don't want to know or that they have already formulated their opinions about all of this. I don't know, it's very hard to figure that out sometimes. What I do know for sure is that I miss them terribly. That's something that I can never really put into words. Its an enormous sense of loss; an emotion that you just never, ever get past. I still cry over what I have missed with them in the last few years. Still cry to this day. I guess what they fail to realize is that I miss them so, so much. It's weird, it's not like if I were home, I would be in every minute of each of their days. It's just that

I feel so detached from them right now. I don't feel connected to anything that they do anymore. I used to see them stressing out studying for a big test, help them with their ties for an awards dinner or a school dance, watch them be ecstatic after winning a big game or scoring a pivotal goal. Even sitting at home with them watching an Islander's game. I miss them in my day and me being in theirs I guess.

"It's weird too, communication with your children that is. It seems like the only acceptable form of communication these days is text messaging. Oh my God, I remember texting back and forth one day with my son and somehow or someway, I ended up texting in all capital letters. Wouldn't you know it, he texts back to me, 'Dad, why are you yelling at me!' Yelling? Holy crap, I'm not even actually talking much less yelling! Ya' know, I'm really not sure if it's their ages or if they harbor so much animosity that they don't really want to keep in touch with me. If I think about it though, just how much time and conversation are 18 and 16 year olds actually having with their parents anyway? I guess I instinctively lean towards the fact that they don't want anything to do with me, but who knows, maybe that's just part of it. I don't know, I really don't know.

"I think that boys in general kind of keep shit to themselves. I think that they don't readily express their emotions on a subject, that is, unless they are really pushed to say what's on their minds. When that happens, you better be ready for the response. That is when you will be the witness to the most utterly raw emotions that you will probably ever experience. When emotions run high, especially built up emotions, you can always expect the truth and nothing but the truth. In hindsight, I wish things never had to get to that point, but that was what happened and I guess it happened for a reason.

"Communication is always tough when you're living apart from your children. I can't tell you how many times I have called their cell phones as well as the house phone; only to leave yet another message that usually went unanswered. That still kills me. Deep down I know that their cell phones almost never leave their bodies. I mean if it isn't in their pocket, it's in their hands. If it isn't in their hands, you can bet the barn that it isn't too far from where they are. Like when I call the house to talk to them at 8:30 – 9:00 at night, you know that everyone is usually sitting on the couch in the den watching something on TV. But when I call at that time, the phone just rings and rings until the machine picks up. Oh my God, I know that for the most part, they are so close that they can hear the phone ringing or see it's me calling from the Caller ID and then they can hear my voice on the machine, but for some reason, no one answers the phone. C'mon guys, I'm not a telemarketer, I'm your dad! That is so upsetting to me; that breaks apart me like nothing else does!"

Chris took a very long pause at this point. It was another one of those pauses where he would turn away from me and look off into the distance. His exhaustive and painful dialogue, which I had dared not interrupt, left him spent. I expected the tears to form. My hunch was correct. Chris looked out into the sparsely populated parkland and wiped the few tears that had swelled under his glasses in the corners of his eyes.

For a moment my head dropped and I too was speechless. I couldn't imagine the feelings that were now bestowed upon him. He was a person I have grown very fond of. He was a good guy. I now felt my own wave of emotion. There remained a moment of awkward silence. The only sound was that of him sniffling between his tears. It actually hurt to look at him sitting there, feeling so isolated from the life that used to be his. Now he removed his glasses as they were obviously fogged. It was awkward; I could see how bad he was hurting. Honestly, I didn't know what to say, didn't know what to do. Other than a hearing those few short sniffles, I felt as if I could hear a pin drop.

Thankfully he composed himself and broke the silence "Let's face it," he continued. "No matter the circumstances, the dad will almost always suffer in silence." His voice faded off with obvious emotion as he choked back more tears. He is alone. I'm willing to bet that that is something that no one really understands. My dad always used to say, 'You know, I may not be too smart, but I ain't too dumb either.' I really feel like I'm "dead on" with this one Dave.

"Men go through a lot of emotions when their lives change so dramatically. We all get used to the way our lives become; we get comfortable in our own skin. When that is no longer there, it can be very, very challenging. I guess we're not expected to face that fear. Guess it's not "manly" enough. I really believe that what I say is the God's honest truth. Our lives change drastically in a very short period of time. It can be overwhelming, really it can. I mean, you go from a four-bedroom colonial in a great neighborhood to a one-bedroom basement apartment in a place that you never even wanted to drive past with your kids in the car. Your fucking wallet is filled with plastic now, not paper, and you max out those credit cards as if you have a gambling problem. It sucks! It really sucks. I mean, look at me; I'm in my early 50's now. Will I ever get the chance to own another home? Will I ever mow my own lawn again? What kind of a fucking life will I live paying someone else's mortgage by renting their basement apartment? If you're going to write anything Dave, tell the world just how much that SUCKS for a guy!"

A man can sound redundant at a time of emotional upheaval. Yet, I listened to Chris as if it was the first time. He held his life so close to his heart. He raised his voice as if his last statement was some sort of a battle cry. He was agitated, waving his finger and his stare took aim directly into my eyes.

"No, really Dave, this needs to be said. Write this down. I know most people see this as an afterthought if it is even a thought at all, but seriously, this needs to be written down. We walk away from everything! If we don't walk away from it, we are forced to give it away. If we're not forced to give it away, it is taken from us in the "negotiations." I always believed that you're not giving it just to your ex-wife, but that you are also giving it to your kids as well. People have to realize though that it is hard on men. It's hard on everyone; except of course, the fucking lawyers."

Chris caught himself and he quickly digressed back to his normal demeanor. His undeniable hurt had gotten the better of him for a few moments there. It was amazing watching him go from solemn tears to unleashing a borderline rage in a few fleeting moments. He scanned the full gamut of emotions. He paused as if to retreat from another tirade.

His reaction about the kids was interesting. What did he really expect? Unless the mother flat out cheats on her husband and throws the dad out, the kids will always hold a stronger allegiance towards their mom. Their mom is the one who nurtures them. Again, it didn't help that his children knew of his infidelity.

He shook his head and looked off into the distance as he continued to speak, "I lived with my mom for about 6 or 7 months in her tiny apartment because I just couldn't afford my own place at that moment. It was humiliating, as a grown man, to have no choice but to move back in with your mother."

"Wait a minute. Let's remember why we are here. Are you speculating that you might be a victim, Chris?"

He took a sip of his soda and did not respond immediately as if he was contemplating an answer.

"Well, maybe not a so called 'victim' in the true sense of the word, but you have to admit, I am paying a very dear price, don't you think, Dave?" His question caught me slightly off guard. I don't know if he was actually expecting me to answer or if the statement was rhetorical.

Nevertheless, I did not cut Chris off because I knew he was a man that liked to continue without being interrupted because not finishing would cause him more anxiety. Without trying to be funny it was apparent that anxiousness only made him twitch his right jaw. And Chris was biased to his own beliefs.

"I don't think it's fair on both fronts." His thoughts wandering, "Why did the kids have to know so much about what happened?"

"C'mon," I interjected, did you really expect the woman that you emotionally knocked out cold was going to hold that one back? Besides it was something that, as you said earlier, was unforgivable. She gave them something they wouldn't forgive you for; for now, at least."

"A woman scorned."

"I hate to say it Chris, but in this instance, I don't think she was the least bit wrong."

"Well, you're certainly entitled to your opinion," he stated indignantly. "But isn't it true by putting the kids in the middle of a conflict with a spouse, it's more likely to affect them in the separation process? Don't the children instinctively start 'to take sides' so to speak?" Of course he was right in that regard, but all I was trying to explain to him was that his soon to be ex-wife did not have any obligation to cover for him.

It was a bomb dropped on her; several bombs to be more precise. Besides the arguments that followed the disclosure, it was not that hard for the boys to decipher what had happened between their parents.

"It's the resentment," he continued. "They aren't even in the middle. They are almost against me to the point where if they aren't put on the spot they don't even want to spend time with me."

"C'mon, Chris. You had to know it wasn't going to be smooth sailing. It's going to take time, probably a very long time at that."

The big guy took his mitt from the soda can and stretched his leg up onto the picnic bench. I didn't have half the physical problems he had experienced but nevertheless my legs and ass cheeks were feeling uncomfortable so I followed suit. I wasn't as big as Chris but I wasn't exactly suited for long hours on park benches either. I got a funny thought as we both scrambled for some sense of comfort. It was like a sitcom; two middle-aged men, in old jeans and tee-shirts sitting together discussing their woes. Then again sitcoms are supposed to be funny, aren't they? There was no humor to be found in this discussion.

"Listen," Chris said, "Christmas was the absolute worst-- no matter what happened I was not a monster. I did not need to be treated the way they treated me."

"How so?"

"They decided they wanted to spend both Christmas Eve and Christmas Day with their mother."

"Wow," I said.

Chris, the big tough guy, proved to me the reputation of his gentle side as his eyes watered again. He removed his glasses and wiped them on his t-shirt. His thoughts seemingly started to drift again, "My son said, 'You're my present dad. Come home for Christmas.'"

"How did that make you feel?" He stared off at the playground to the far left.

"How do you think it made me feel? Oh my God, it shattered me! I remember vividly feeling the thrust of emotions from his softly spoken innocent words. But I had to tell him the truth. I had to explain to him that just because it was Christmas, my coming home wouldn't solve the issues that were before us. I had caused so much hurt, and that it would take a very long time for it to heal, if ever.

"Sometimes the words of a child can make you appreciate the innocence and simplicity of their thought process. If only life remained that simple.

"'But you're alone,' my son said. "I didn't answer but I wanted to tell him that of course I'm alone. There's no one around. But I have to suffer in silence. This was going to be my penance. Going back was just not an option."

Chris was pensive as he reached for that spot of hair that he was tweaking earlier. "That was it. The boys, especially my eldest, decided that they would see me Christmas Day for one hour – not even dinner. They would see my mother when they saw me. No separate visit. My mother thought they were having dinner with us and it just broke her heart. The plans changed so rapidly, and with it being the holiday and all, it just seemed so devastating. It was as if they were punishing her because of me. She didn't have anything to do with the whole mess. But it's just the natural progression of divorce. Everyone is affected. Each of us is a casualty of divorce I guess.

"Brother-in-laws, sister-in-law's and friends in common that I shared so many laughs and so many beers with throughout the years, now fail to even acknowledge your existence when you are in the same place at the same time. The last time I saw my in-laws at one of the kid's games, my father-in-law politely acknowledged my 'Hello,' but then turned to me and handed me a pile of mail that my wife had given to him to pass along to me. What was that all about? You really can't take five seconds and hand me my mail yourself? The whole business was just so strange. I guess there's no book on how to act to your grandchildren's father when things go wrong between you and his daughter. I know I wish my mother had one of those books to read!" I know what kind of father and what kind of son Chris is. I know it was extremely tough on him and though it all began with his indiscretion, I could not feel anything less than sympathy, for him, his family, his children, and his wife. Yet how do I confess that to a man that has lost feelings for a woman he has spent the last twenty-five years of his life with?

I knew that Chris was in the "father business" from day one. Changing diapers so willingly, making bottles, dressing them in cute outfits, and taking the kids everywhere he went. Shopping, doctor's appointments, school field trips, 'class mom' shit and spending hours in parks like the one we were now sitting in. He carried around that diaper bag on his shoulder as proudly as a warrior would wear his sword. I thought about our fathers, how unimaginable; a generation of males that never even thought about doing such womanly things. But Chris didn't just adapt to it, he loved it, he really did.

"I'll be right back." Chris stated. He returned a few minutes later with a big basket of fries for us to share along with two more sodas. "Might as well add more junk to this poor man's feast," he said with a big smile. He pulled open a package of ketchup and squirted its contents just on his side of the plate. Neither of us spoke just then, instead we dipped our burnt fries into the condiment and nibbled away. He eventually continued between bites of the fries, "That was it for me Dave. I was a bumbling mess. My mother felt horrible having to watch her sons' obvious disappointment." It was his fault that his mother and brother were not going to see the boys for Christmas, and he knew it. "It was very difficult to keep it together at that time. A pathetic loser I was. I could be amongst 1000 people, but still I felt so alone. Thank God for family; my mom, my dad, my brother."

Chris was another familiar statistic, also the product of divorce. He never asked his dad but I'm sure he wondered if the old man went through the same series of emotions.

It's hard to imagine but Chris confessed to not only finding himself crying frequently when alone, but when he was with family he would retreat to the bathroom and run the water or flush the toilet to distract the noise of his sobs. He said that he learned to cry so silently during these days. Here is a guy who could have taken one long swipe at me from the other side of the table and knocked me into the grass without even standing up.

He returned to the Christmas conversation. "You know, I was always the one taking all the photos on Christmas morning. I wouldn't open my own gifts till I got those perfect pictures of my family."

I took a sip of my soda with the hope of enticing him to do the same; to take a break from the painful memories. But a quick sip and he continued, "I had that camera in my hand for all their games, birthdays, and any family function that I felt demanded to be captured in time. I would go to all those elementary school chorus concerts, you know the ones that were only four songs and twenty minutes long, and I would shoot over 100 pictures of my son belting out a remake of a show tune for the masses! I would shoot all my neighbors' kids too and give them a disc the next day with the images of their child singing their hearts out either at the top of their lungs or with barely a whisper. Some I swore would even just lip synch! It was crazy; you would think that the concert was two hours long!"

"I've seen many of your photos buddy...no doubt you are good. You shouldn't obliterate those memories Chris. They are a part of your life; a good part. You could certainly remember the bad. But you don't need to make a list. You know why you're here. You know if your marriage was solid, you wouldn't be here."

He bypassed my comments as if I never even said them. "Concentrated on sports photography for a while too," he said. "Had a lot of practice shooting sports with three great athletes in the family."

Chris lifted his right forefinger, tucking it under his glasses to rub his eye. "I took some fantastic shots of the boys playing the sports that they loved," he said as he drifted off and stared away in the distance. He was repeating himself but part of the exercise was the allowance to vent.

"The boys will come around soon," I said. But I knew as soon as I said that, it was all bullshit. It wasn't going to be soon. It was going to take a lot of time for those kids to warm up to their father. He hurt them, he hurt them bad and he hurt their mother too. They had many nights where they heard her cry through her closed bedroom door, or in the middle of the day for seemingly no reason at all. He was responsible for all that and so much more. They weren't going to forget any of that pain for a long time to come.

That was the reality, and with the passage of the time, up till now there has not been much progress in the positive column.

"We will see," he said. "We're talking about a dad that went to all their games, even stayed for all of their practices to watch what they were learning." Trailing off he said, "Now, they say to me that they have a ride. Or I could meet them there. Or that their mom wanted to take them that day. I remembered a line from a book by Mitch Albom. I think it was called, 'For One More Day." He told of a character receiving pictures in the mail of his daughter's wedding which had recently passed, and that he wasn't invited to. He said, 'Where I used to be invited, I was now notified.' That's still so hard to swallow, very hard to swallow."

My silent opinion reiterated that those who claim children are resilient to divorce are full of crap. They aren't. Couples want to convince themselves of that so to alleviate their guilt. Kids adjust because they have to, not because they get over their parents divorcing. Still, I don't believe that couples should stay together just for the kid's sake. If the home is filled with constant turmoil and arguing that doesn't cease then it is probably time for one spouse to leave; if not for a little while, then permanently.

Chris fingered the last of his fries. "Do you know how much shit I still take?" he said. "Not only from her, but from the kids. And my older one seems as if he can speak for the other two. 'We can't see you today,' he will decide..."

"Again my friend, you certainly do not have to convince me of your adoration for the kids. I know you were a great father." I paused so not to try and knock him out. "But, you did cheat--and you got caught."

"I know, but when is enough, enough? When do I begin to be forgiven and everyone begins to inch slightly forward? To accept it for what it is?" Now he stretched his chin out, as if his collar was too tight.

"When they're ready," I said.

"Almost two years already. I even asked my wife if the boys would be willing to speak to a therapist. 'That isn't going to work' she said to me."

I didn't know how many times I was going to have to repeat myself, but they resented him, plain and simple. There are consequences for our actions. Chris appeared ready to move onto another touchy subject; money.

"There just never seems to be enough money. I've left the house and did not ask her to sell it. I didn't want to uproot my children. She works too for Christ's sake and yet I even help her pay the mortgage. Do they not appreciate this?"

"Maybe there is a possibility the kids don't even understand that?"

"She actually said she was putting the divorce off as much as she could because she can't afford to get divorced and lose the money and the benefits. Not only that, she said she would actually take me back."

"Unbelievable; but your right on with this too Chris. With the divorce pending she has to be somewhat fair and let you go.

"I do have what you will think is a stupid question. Do you miss her at all?"

"No. I don't think that I do. She could be very controlling at times, understandably even more so towards the end. I'm sure though that she would disagree with that statement; telling you that it only came later in our marriage, when she had her suspicions. We argued a lot. Over really stupid shit, too. I would tell her that she was 'getting her Irish up'."

Chris mockingly twirled his forefinger. "She would go round and round about the same thing over and over again. Don't get me wrong; I do miss the good times as much as anyone else. The holidays, the family trips, etc. but realistically, how do I reconcile with a person that I would argue with three minutes into any conversation?" Chris stuck his left hand straight out. "See how steady? When I get off the phone with her it's like this." He shook his hand fast, sideways. "Shaking like a leaf," he said.

"How is it for you now that you don't have anyone in your life?" I asked bluntly.

He took a moment and dug deeply for his reply. "I guess I didn't realize how incredibly lonely I would be. I thought the boys would always be around; at least in some capacity.

At least that would have given me a sense of solace. Sometimes it's even worse than in the beginning because I am further away from any kind of peace."

"Are you moving on a little?"

"Well, I finally got my own place. It's small but I have my privacy."

"Good for you!" I said. I was happy for Chris. It was indeed time for him to move on in his own right.

"I didn't need anything bigger for financial reasons. I would have done my best to get something a little roomier. I just couldn't afford it."

"Why," I asked.

"For the kids, of course. But I knew very early that they wouldn't stay over. My oldest son told me as much.

'Dad, get real. It's just not our home.'"

Etched on his face was incredible pain, "Dave, I'm actually somewhat embarrassed to bring someone into my mini home. It's too small for me. I always feel closed in, like I can't breathe. It sucks."

"Naturally, I know how terrible you feel," I said. "But actually recording it for the readers---"

"Don't worry about that," He cut in. "After all I agreed 100% percent to do this...Misery loves company, maybe someone out there can relate to that feeling too."

"Do you ever hear from her?" I asked. We agreed not to use names so he knew I would never refer to her by her name.

"You know it can be very frustrating when you argue over the phone. And now I have to resort to text messages and e-mails. It's so fu - friggin' ludicrous." Thankfully he refrained from cursing in diatribe.

"Are you staying busy?" I asked this because I believed too much alone time would add to his mounting anxiety. I of course knew, absolutely, that he would never do anything stupid, but I still thought something that would take his time up a little would benefit him.

"I think you remember," he said. "I had a lot of time off because I got hurt at work. I had some surgery. But I'm back now. Working a sector car again, and dealing with all the bullshit that comes along with it."

"At least you're getting all of your old parts fixed before you retire," I joked.

"True. But you know when you fix so many things on that old car, sometimes it's just better to go out and buy a new one!"

I thought for a minute; this poor bastard not only has to endure being ignored by his kids, his continuous resentment from his wife, his financial problems, that he confessed to being more than frail, and physical ailments to boot. I do confess that I sincerely believe it is time for his ex to let up and understand that an unfortunate end came to their marriage, but Chris is really trying to do the right thing.

Chris genuflected on his passion for photography.

"I think I might go to the beach and take some photos of the water and the waves. Maybe get out there really early and get a few action shots of some surfers. That's not something that you see every day. I'm sure I'll be talking with some of them after the tides change. Ya' know, 'Hey where can I get a copy of those pictures dude?' Still I do get to shoot pictures at my sons' games, even though I have to sit far away and usually by myself."

I remarked about the beach idea because I thought it was a good place for him to clear his head. "Good idea buddy. I think being out in the fresh air will help a lot...what about maybe going out on a date?"

Chris smirked, "I don't know. I haven't been out there, so to speak, and to be honest with you, I'm really not into that at all. I hate the way I look and I hate the way I feel. Besides, from what I hear from people who are doing that, people my age are absolutely crazy! Men and women; just friggin' crazy. I really don't have the head for that."

"But---"

"But what about the one I was with? Stop right there, I already told you that it didn't become what I had hoped that it would become."

"You're an interesting guy," I said.

"An interesting guy who is losing everything...Of course I always want to take care of the kids, but I'm not even divorced yet and I'm already paying the mortgage and child support. Together it causes me to live in a basement apartment and pay someone else's mortgage."

I laughed because I felt humor needed to be injected to quell the misery. Still there would always remain the mantra for Chris. 'You made your bed, now lie in it.'

"Looking forward, what do you think could be in store for you?" I asked..." What will you be searching for?"

"Certainly I wish for a better relationship with my boys, especially since we had been pretty close. I would also like to be debt free." Again, we laughed especially when Chris cracked that wide grin after a comment required it. "I am paying out so much now and like I said the divorce isn't even final. The courts are so one sided it's disgusting. It's not like my wife is destitute."

"I have to agree with you their buddy." And though I felt bad for many women there certainly were the ones who reveled in destroying their husbands.

Chris ran his hand through his neatly buzzed hair. "I don't know buddy, maybe divorce is in the genes, like a disease...But I'll tell you something for sure. There isn't a shot in hell that I would go through this again. I have my children so there is no reason to get married."

"I guess if you have companionship you know go to the movies, to dinner, get some every now and again---that's all we could ask for, especially at our age." We laughed again.

"Dave, now it's my turn to ask you a question. Do you believe that a woman could possibly believe what a man could go through during a divorce, regardless of who made the decision?"

"I think, and it's only my opinion, that women could be so tied up with the idea that the man is now free to do what he wants. Go out whenever they wanted to; come home whenever they wanted to, not having to worry about childcare. Not worrying about her while she tends to the kids, works, cleans the house, etc....I believe they could hurt, but there has to be some kind of resentment for the lack of freedom they must endure."

"I really wish that they would open their minds a little,"

Chris said. "Because barring moving right in with another woman, the pain of loneliness and distance from your kids can be devastating...I take that back. Even if I did move in with someone I probably will still feel 95% of what I'm feeling right now. That feeling of not having your children in your life because they don't want you in theirs is too much for me to absorb sometimes."

"Agreed." I seemed to be flip-flopping on going back and forth with my own ideas. Chris seemed exhausted. I selfishly asked him if he would like to continue another day. But he was willing to stick it out. "The sun is still up, let's just keep talking," he said.

I was committed to listening and have my buddy vent. His marital discord seemed to be as difficult as being pummeled in a fistfight, so I wanted to interject questions of good memories. I asked about his honeymoon and his relationship with his wife during better times.

"Ah, my honeymoon," he recalled. "By the way did you know Michael was on his honeymoon a week before mine; same place too.

"He left me a note congratulating me and telling me what to do and what not to do. It was funny, getting to the front desk in another part of the world and find a letter waiting for you!"

"I didn't know that. It's a small, small world."

Chris lifted his glasses back to the bridge of his nose. "We were like teenagers." He seemed to smile recalling better times. "We had a blast on our honeymoon. We participated in all the games at the resort. Toga parties, which by the way I remember wanting to slide my hand under her sheet. There was beach volleyball, karaoke, pool games, drinking games, a lot of fun stuff.

"Then after a while, we settled into our home, decided to

become parents and eventually brought three beautiful kids into this world. I went to all the Ob-Gyn appointments and I was there for all the sonograms. I even had the sonogram pictures laminated and showed them off as an actual 'picture' of my kid. One of my sons' were born on the first day of my annual vacation pick. Talk about timing; it was just right! Tears flowed from my eyes when each of my sons was born. We were a family. We had our good times and had our bad times. Some of those bad times stayed longer than expected and then tragically and sadly I might add, it all just fell apart."

"Do you remember when?" I asked. "Is there anything you would have done differently?"

"Of course there are always regrets. I guess if I had to go back and look at what went wrong, I would have to say that there was a breakdown in communication between us. She was the 'driving it home' type while I was the one who would shut up and keep it to myself. I would always tell her that I argue with people all day at work, the last place that I want to continue arguing is my own home. That would eventually change too.

"I could have been more honest with her. I should have said something when I first started to feel it slip away. I don't know why I didn't; maybe I just didn't want to. I really don't know. At the end of the day, back then, I wasn't honest and that hurt a lot of people that I really cared about. It hurt people in every corner of my life. I became numb. I used to say that I felt like a chalk line of a human being, like in the old time 'crime scenes' that you used to see on episodes of Dragnet or Adam 12. I was completely void of any emotion. I would go through the motions with my eyes closed. I don't know, if I didn't face it, I didn't have to deal with it. That was the wrong approach. You know, it was scary too. Even though, at times, it may not be the best situation, we still are so afraid to leave our comfort zones. I know that I was. I think anyone who says that they're not is full of shit.

"We get into little grooves in our lives and we snuggle into them for comfort, protection and shelter to ride out the little storms that we encounter in our days. But when is enough, enough? I guess we should always re-evaluate our own self-worth every now and again. I didn't do that, but then neither did she. I don't know Dave there are no books that tell us how to be a good husband or how to be a good wife. The same with being parents; no one has written books on how to master those skills. We wing it. We try to do the best that we can do. I kept everything inside of me. I always did. It started to produce resentment and I went elsewhere to make me feel like more of a person to myself.

"I liked that feeling of feeling new again, it consumed me. I derived so much comfort from it; comfort that I really needed to feel. I believed at the time that my new 'friend' truly cared for me; I could see that she genuinely did. I thought that this is what I deserved for myself. I forget to finish the other part of my life though. Maybe if I had been honest earlier, this would have had a different ending. I don't know, I just don't know. As painful as it is, I just didn't feel it for my wife anymore. At that point, I just could not get the love back for her. I tried inside of me but realized that I was trying for the wrong reasons. I wasn't happy and that should be worth something.

"I know there are a fairly high percentage of men who regret getting divorced. It changes everything about you; everything. You have to charge everything because you quickly become 'cash poor.' You never have enough. You buy store brands instead of name brands. Everything changes, everything just changes so fast in your life and it's forever. You don't even have time to realize what the hell is happening to you. You have to rely on yourself more than anyone else. You are it. It's just you, my man. It's just you in your lonely, pathetic world. The stress of a marital separation is overwhelming.

"It affects your health in many bad ways. I ate like shit and it showed. I just neglected to take care of myself. I was breaking down, usually from the inside out. I can usually handle stress. I deal with it at work almost all the time. But this stress is different. The stress that is thrust on you when going through a divorce is nothing like the stress at work. It truly tears you apart. My life was in total chaos. You don't sleep, you stay up all night staring at the ceiling just thinking and thinking and wondering how you will you get through this, and what is going to be left of you once you do get to the other side.

"You are always tired. Every single person that you ask for advice has a different opinion. Your health suffers, your finances suffer, and you eat more and exercise less. If you smoke, you'll smoke more. If you drink, you'll drink more. All of your vices are amplified to try to deal with the hand that you now hold. You never have the option of folding your hand either. You are forced to play every card that you are dealt; and I can assure you that you are not coming out of this a winner by any means. It just hits you from every angle, and usually at the same time.

"I'll admit, I wasn't prepared for that, I really wasn't. When all that stress knocked at my door, I was simply not ready for what was on the other side of it.

Your health suffers immensely. You gain weight and you don't do anything to reverse that course. You let yourself go and the stress just keeps coming; hitting you harder and harder with each connecting punch.

"It was so detrimental to me. I'm still feeling the effects of not being prepared for it. You start to feel bad for yourself. You make your own 'pity party.' You want everyone to feel sorry for you and your situation. In hindsight, that is not the way to go. Expect the worst and deal with it as it comes your way. Your life is completely different from what is once was just a short time ago. Your life officially sucks. You no longer have any money to burn. You borrow to pay what needs to be paid. You are a totally different person. Wake up fool! This is your life now. Get fucking used to it! Snap out of it and snap out of it fast!

"You cannot afford to lie down and play dead because the stress of this will kill you; it literally will. Your blood pressure goes higher and your waistline gets wider. You have to deal with each situation as it arises. Make up your mind; make your decisions and act on them. Don't keep wallowing in your own self - pity. You need to stop being pathetic, man up and handle this! Don't sit there and cry now; you wanted this and you have so many other people looking at you and waiting for you to find a definitive answer and make a definitive decision. You hold other peoples' lives in the balance, and they are so adversely affected either by your decisions, or by your inability to make one. It is by far the most difficult time in your life and it is obviously the most stressful too. The quicker that you realize that, the better off you will handle it or at least respond to it. I didn't do that; I did nothing; thinking that it was going to just work itself out. I'm here to tell you folks that it does not work that way.

"A very good friend of mine would always remind me of something. He would always say, "If nothing changes, nothing changes." Truer words have never been spoken. No one is going to do this for you. I was wrong, I refused to take command of my situation and it consumed me. In the long run, it cost me dearly; both in the financial sense and more profoundly in the emotional sense. You lose your self – respect, your dignity and your self – worth. You silently lose the respect of others to the point where people don't really want to be around you anymore. They quickly become tired of your 'patheticness' of you always asking for advice yet never acting on any of it. They get tired of the way that you are, and the state that you are in, and the fact that you are not looking to help yourself, but to only 'talk' about what you're going to do to better your situation. You do nothing about your current state of affairs and they become tired of your self - inflicted pity parties. You get depressed, you start to get apathetic to everything in your life, you look like shit and slowly but surely, you find yourself increasingly alone."

I got it. He had vented plenty of noticeable chaos. He poured his heart out. Chris was still feeling somewhat ill, he confessed. He still cried at moments of darkness alone in his apartment. He still had that pit in his stomach. He painstakingly described a moment a long time ago, when he was at that breaking point where everything was coming down around him. He said that it was when the four walls started to collapse, the floor ended up giving out too. He was helpless. He recalled with bone chilling detail, just how he thought about ending all of his pain. I don't want to quote him here, for it was just too difficult watching him reflect that moment to me. I will respect his wish and instead paraphrase his fatal thoughts in text. It was that moment he said when you couldn't even think that you will never have anything good happen in your life again. It is, as he called it, a "very dark day." He actually thought of ending the sinking ship that had become his life. His thoughts were of his hopelessness.

His doubted he would ever be able to get out of the debt he now found himself in. His thoughts tormented him as to his impending loneliness of no longer having his children in his world on a daily basis. Of waking up alone, eating dinner alone, going places alone. Everything from this point would be done alone. "Sleeping in a house alone, in the dark, is the feeling of profound emptiness. It's almost unbearable," he said.

Chris went on to describe the set-up in his bed; he placed a many times folded bath towel on the bed and he laid down on that towel, making sure that it lies strategically behind his heart. He went on to describe getting yet another many times folded towel and placing that one upon his chest, directly over his heart with his left hand. He had chosen the darkest colored towels he owned; one was a sandy shade of brown, while the other towel, a royal blue. In his right hand he gripped his service weapon, seemingly in position to finish his plan. His thoughts were to minimize the blood pool by allowing the towels to absorb the blood from the hole that he inflicted in his heart until it altogether stopped pumping. He never executed his plan; or himself for that matter. He re-evaluated his self- worth and realized that even in his darkest moment, he was better than what he had planned for himself. What would that solve? He admitted, through his tears, that this was a very critical moment in this process; the thought of one of his family members finding him or a fellow police officer bearing witness to the results of his final moment of utter despair. Taking his life was not the road to travel. Despite the feelings of loneliness and complete loss of control in almost every aspect of his life, he wisely chose to ride out the storm. It was indeed a horrific storm and he made certain to tell me that it has yet to pass through his life completely; that is, if it ever actually does. Thankfully things have been getting a little better with the passage of time. "This too shall pass," he said. There are a large percentage of those who would not feel any sympathy for Chris. After all, infidelity is a huge betrayal for anyone. But it does take two to tango. A man could also feel his wife just doesn't respect him any longer.

Chris continued, "How much punishment does a man deserve for his indiscretions? Is there ever a point where someone says, 'OK, you have hereby suffered enough, now go forth my son and make your life a meaningful one.' No, there most certainly is not.

"Your choices dictate the remainder of your life. Unfortunately, at this stage of the game, you literally have more years behind you than you do in front of you. You are burdened with the pains, which you have most likely caused yourself; pains which you have brought upon yourself and on those who loved you the most. You are now relegated to live your life somewhat incomplete, to always have within you, even the smallest sense of an emotional void. If you're one of the lucky ones, you can find happiness in a person who can forgive you for your past, and who can realize that you are human, and readily capable of imperfection and mistakes.

"Forgiveness must first come for yourself, for your faults, and how they have adversely affected those around you. If you are ever to find some resemblance of inner peace and happiness again in your life, you will need to stand tall, accept your mistakes and make things right with those who you have wronged.

"The problem becomes even more complicated when those who you need to make amends with, refuse to accept your plea for their forgiveness. That is what will leave you in a dark and hollow emotional abyss that you can never transcend from; for forgiveness to truly be awarded, all involved must first be on the same page. The first step to forgiveness is the willingness to forgive. Forgiveness is constantly being heralded in the world as a means for someone to release themselves from the chains of resentment & retaliation. You can read of it in many, many books, especially the ultimate literary work; The Bible. Archbishop Desmond Tutu was once quoted as saying, "Forgiveness says that you are giving another chance to a new beginning." You should always remember also that sometimes you forgive people simply because you want them in your life. I have never met a perfect man, or a perfect woman for that matter. People can change. Look at their reasons for changing; some may very well surprise you. Some will do it out of the recognition of their mistakes in their life, others for more selfish and shallow reasoning. If you truly know the person seeking your forgiveness, then take a long deep look at their request and decide if you feel that they have truly learned from their mistakes. Give them another chance to get it right. Don't worry, your guard will be up and you will subconsciously always be protecting yourself from this person hurting you again. But at the end of the day, you will know if they are sincere; you will feel it. This I can promise you. I recently finished reading the book, The Dark Devine by Bree Despain. In it, she explores one of the many virtues of forgiveness with this quote; "We don't forgive people because they deserve it. We forgive them because they need it – because we need it." This is so true."

Chris sat straight on the bench again, his legs forward. Maybe his back was bothering him. He folded his hands and smiled at me.

"It is what it is. I just need to go to work, do things I enjoy, keep busy and of course, always keep trying and trying and trying to mend my relationship with the kids, although how much can a man take; how much do I concede to them without ultimately having them lose respect for me? I need to somehow reinvent myself for the time that I am to remain on this earth."

It was hard to answer that one so I gestured hunching my shoulders up, I don't know. I was glad though that Chris was continuing his hobbies and still does some charity work, giving back to the community. He always liked doing things for someone who he knew could never repay him. He said that it kept him busy. It kept his mind from thinking about all the other things in his life. He was even able to befriend some local radio personalities to help further the causes that he undertook. Chris exhaled. "I realize I don't deserve much sympathy, but contrary to belief I still tried to do the right thing. I didn't insist on selling the house. I still give plenty of money for her and the kids to live...and I did the best I could do when I lived at home, many times I felt, with no appreciation for most of it."

I didn't want to become redundant, but I wanted to reiterate that it was going to take time, and that I really believe if he hung in there without any more obstacles, things would eventually start to get better.

I am a believer in children never getting over divorce, but with the right parenting on both of the couple's parts, they can certainly adjust. "That was the hard part," he said, pointing his finger at me as he spoke.

He changed gears and told me, "Dave, I don't think that the scorned parties could disengage themselves from the marriage until they find some sense of forgiveness."

"There has to be a realization that you will always be your children's father and that she will always be their mother.

"After all, you will always share in the lives of your children. There are graduations, weddings, grandkids; it never ends. We, as our children's parents, will always be in their lives."

I waited for Chris to respond, but he just looked away. I continued. "Just think if the shoe was on the other foot and your wife was the one who strayed. You would be devastated. And the children would be just as devastated and would treat her the way they are treating you."

"You're 100% right. I blindsided them not fully aware of the consequences."

"Acknowledgment is always a good thing, Chris."

"And now," he said. "I'm being blindsided both personally and financially... I still get my balls broken regardless if I pay for this expense and that expense, the school and sports expenses and everything I can. I still get grief."

"I'm not going to reiterate everything Chris, especially now on paper where the reader will feel slighted with redundancy. I know what you're doing to make things easier. I know what you have given up. But again---"

"OK, you made your point," he said, running his hand through his hair again, stopping for a second on that crown.

"I can tell you this; I will never go through this bullshit again. I might take someone out to dinner, maybe even listen to their whining regarding their own baggage, but marry? Never! Would you believe, I don't go to bars and clubs alone, not my thing; it never was. I don't have the time or energy for it. I'm not interested in any of it. None of it!"

"You don't go out at all?" I asked.

"No, sometimes I do. But it's only to meet a few friends or attend an event. It's expensive. Twelve bucks a drink! Are they crazy? For what? I just have a hard time wrapping my head around all that right now, I'm sorry." He was laughing as if it were an unimaginable institution.

Chris was a guy who could always laugh out loud. If you didn't have a personal relationship with him, you would never know if anything was bothering him.

"Well, I still think there is hope my friend," I said. "That's all we could imagine. Don't think I haven't gone out spent 100 bucks on dinner and got a kiss on the cheek at the end, without any promise of another date. That's life."

"Nope. Sorry Dave, I'll have no part of that. Sorry man, not happening."

"Don't worry about that," I said as we both laughed at how indignant he was to the social scene.

"It's really hard for me," Chris said. "Sometimes it's just mass hysteria for me. I think and I think, and I rethink my entire life up until this very moment. And I try not to vent, although I've made up for that by talking to you today." He smiled and shook his head. "It's not supposed to be in a man's chemical make-up to be soft, to be heartbroken..."

"I hope this at least might have been some help to you. I would hope that your anxiety does not become a detriment to your health."

"I have felt like I was about to have a heart attack."

"I'm sure you have. Divorce is as life changing as a death."

"Always could be worse. I had a friend who married his childhood sweetheart. Through all their problems his love never wavered. After close to 17 years of marriage she had an affair and left him. They had no kids so he was left to fend for himself. He didn't expect it and had no safeguards in place to deal with the problems that this caused him. He went on a backwards diet regiment; eating all kinds of shit. Smoking more and drinking more. He just spun out of control. He grew more and more depressed each and every day. He was getting into trouble at his job. He eventually ate, drank and smoked himself to some very poor health. He just couldn't get over it. It was hard watching my friend self - destruct. All his friends, myself included, tried to get him to reverse his course. He didn't want to hear anything. He just kept falling down a slippery slope. He got diabetes; he suffered from a lot of other medical shit that could have been avoidable. His body just couldn't keep up with the thrashing that he was giving it. His heart stopped working effectively; his organs were tired. He eventually just got so sick and one day I received a call from one of our common friends that he just died. He let his situation consume him and it cost him his life at a very young age. The only person I knew that I truly believe died of a proverbial broken heart."

I watched Chris as he stared over at the knoll leading to the barbecue pits. His separation was going on for too long. He needed the legal closure.

Chris humbled me. He had impressed me with his forthright conversation, his ability to acknowledge his shortcomings, and his true pain as a parent who might never be accepted by his boys as their perfect dad. Still, after all the honesty, the tears, I wondered what this man was looking for. I was aware he did not believe there was a Cinderella out there for him? He couldn't possibly at his age believe in fairytales. However, he was being unfair not only to himself but to a future prospect. On one hand it seemed as if he was never going to let his guard down, but human nature and a path to some kind of peace would require that we drop our defenses; take that chance.

"I know you didn't love your wife anymore." I was going out on a limb here. "But what did you expect, or rather what are you expecting now? I know you said just companionship, but a romance is a human yearning, and you have to move into one with realistic expectations. You can't live alone forever."

There was a glint of a smile. "No, I don't believe in mermaids and unicorns anymore. But whatever the outcome is here, I just want some definitive sign of closure."

"No one is saying that you have to roll over and play dead. But I have to say after this conversation whether you believe it or not, you are already on your way back. Once the papers are signed, you will see. It will be like a pair of cinder blocks being knocked off your shoulders...The most important thing here is to get it right with your kids. The rest will fall into place."

"This is the hand I was dealt; this is the hand I will play. I'm getting it." Chris said.

"Sort of like it's in God's hands now," I replied.

"True," he replied.

"It has become a throwaway world buddy; televisions, stereos, phones, computers, wives and husbands." We shared a laugh and simultaneously lifted our feet back over the bench. Chris got up and stretched.

"In another generation," he said. "It was simple. Sure problematic, but simple. The men worked, the woman stayed home and raised the kids. They didn't complain about socks on the floor or toothpaste caps."

"Had they had the independence that women have today, it would have been a lot more difficult to iron out their problems. Many women today could live without a husband...And by the way, your parents were divorced."

"Well it was never 'Father Knows Best' anyway I suppose. In real life the whole cast of that show was screwed up."

"I think we're spent Chris. We have covered a multitude of marriage woes but I just want to conclude with a couple of questions that follow this nightmare journey you were on."

"Go ahead," he smiled. "Might as well, we're here now. But in case you're going to ask me, yes my back hurts and yes I'm spent, but no, I do not wish to continue another time. Let's get this done." Then he tossed his soda can into the nearest wastebasket about five feet away. "Swoosh," he shouted.

It was good to see him display a little childlike behavior right before some really tough questions.

"And you're positive you don't have feelings of hurting yourself again?"

"If I did I'd be dead already. Next question."

I pressed on about his wife. "Why did your marriage last as long as it did?"

"First let me say that no one gets married to get divorced, to go through this emotional hell and give the lawyers what's left of your money. I didn't go in thinking it wouldn't last. I really did want to be married. I loved my wife and I thought that would be enough. Secondly, who want to be separated from their children and not watch them grow and learn on a daily basis? It might be one of the main reasons couples stay together, except for finances, which wasn't the case with me..." Again, Chris rubbed his eyes and ran his hand through his hair. At least he didn't have the hairstyle to mess up because he ran his fingers over his head often.

I decided to lighten up before he concluded. I waved my hands out front. "...Again, with the hair and the jaw thing?" I joked.

"Well I need some kind of release," he laughed. "I don't smoke and I barely drink."

"Go ahead Chris, continue."

"Also my house. My house was a home; a warm and safe place to be." Chris smiled faintly and made a pouring gesture. "I was the Breakfast Chef to my kids. I could whip up omelets or One –Eyed Pete's for breakfast like a short order cook. I was the best!"

I didn't respond to Chris' analogy of his home. To me it was just more confusion and mass contradiction. How could he reminisce about a home and so desperately want to leave? I did not feel like getting into it about the facts. I luckily did not have to experience the animosity that exists between Chris and his spouse. Their dislike built to a crescendo that would cause my heart to stop. Still, it isn't unusual. If statistics are correct about the aspects of divorce than they could expect to be angry at each other for years to come.

Chris was wavering in his conversation. "The saddest of course is the children, the extended family, and the circle of friends we shared. Nobody wishes to take sides but it is tough..."

"Chris," I said. "Believe it when I say to you that no matter what happened I sincerely feel for you. Not just because I know you, but you really are a good guy."

"You asked me an extremely difficult question earlier. No, no I would never hurt myself. Yet, in this particular moment in my life, I sometimes wonder if everyone concerned would wish me dead, especially my wife."

"Who knows, maybe one day you could be friends."

He laughed. "Friendship," he said, "with any woman might just be an illusion."

I laughed and Chris smiled at me so I knew there was no insult. "Do you really believe that? About the dying thing I mean." I asked.

"I don't know."

"Don't you think that your children would grieve terribly?

Don't you know that you can still watch over them, see them grow into adults and share their future joys, and guide them through their future sorrows?"

"I haven't thought that far ahead...Would you like something else to eat or drink before the snack stand closes?"

I shook my head, shot my eyes up, no. I felt we were very

close to the end now and I just didn't have the stomach for any more soda, chips or fries. I knew the conversation was just going to include more psychobabble. If I were his therapist I would have made a fortune today. Besides it was clear that Chris was wearing down. Looking straight ahead, then down, then away almost mechanically. A man left to his own accountability. A man that would have to lie in the bed he made.

He looked me in the eye now and squinted revealing apparent discomfort. Chris spoke in almost a whisper, "I just didn't think the kids had to know so soon." "That's it buddy. We are here to discuss what is. The kid's finding out, it is what it is. We are re - entering a world of repeating what is."

"I understand," Chris said.

"I just want you to begin to heal; begin to move on...Again, shit flies both ways. I know men whose wives cheated and they felt compelled to tell their kids that their mother was a whore! Chris I have to hit you with one more difficult question."

"You mean there is a question more difficult than the ones you've already asked?" He laughed out loud again.

"You know when you laugh like that; no one would believe what you are feeling deep down."

"Well then, that's a good thing," he remarked.

"Chris described to me one of the worst days you have had during this whole ordeal."

"Shit," he said. "Other than the suicide moment?" He looked pensive. "One of my worst days? OK. It was around that Christmas we already discussed. But it was afterwards when I was home alone. My mother was out so I could fill myself with anxiety as not to get her worried. First I had one of my usual phone disagreements with my wife. I was holding my head so hard I thought that it was going to explode..." He laughed but nervously. "I walked outside and sat in the dark in my truck. I was breathing so heavy I actually grabbed my chest, hoping it would stop pounding so hard. I started to cry. I was actually crying for what seemed like an eternity. Things would never be the same for me. I prayed for some kind of redemption. I wiped the tears from my face then all of a sudden, the waterworks started again. In my entire life, I never felt so terrible. Will I ever have a good relationship with my kids one day? I mean at my age; will I ever own a house again? Will I ever mow my own lawn again? Will I ever wash my car again in my own driveway? Will I ever get out of this debt that I so quickly got myself into? Will I ever be able to pay back the thousands of dollars that I borrowed from my family members? Jesus Christ, I'm 50 fucking years old! I have more years behind me now than I do in front of me. I just feel like such a friggin' L-O-S-E-R! That was one of my worst moments; I'd have to say.

"I know that Twinkies made a great comeback, but I really think you're looking at a guy whose 'comeback days' are behind him. I may run out of time to do what I want to do in my life. I'm starting over now and trying to accomplish now what took me so, so long to accomplish then. It is, at times, actually at most times, a completely overwhelming feeling; one that I really cannot shake, no matter how hard I try.

Want to hear the worst of it? Am I really any happier than I was before? At this point I would have to give you a resounding "No."

"The thought of that answer makes me want to vomit; it really does Dave. You walk through all of this to reward yourself with the promise of "happiness" and you find yourself no closer to it than when you started. Let me tell you my friend; that truly sucks!"

Chris proved that no matter how big or tough a man is, we are all vulnerable in times of unnerving sadness and the reality of being utterly alone. It wasn't a record of my own life but God knows I have felt the same terrible affliction.

Chris whispered as if he were talking to himself. "My little one still hopes that I'm coming home."

"I know. I know everything now. And you are doing a great service by documenting your experience because it shows that divorce is a terrible thing; even if it is necessary."

The big guy stood again and stretched his arms together way over his head. I chuckled and copied his actions. I needed to stretch myself. I centered both hands on the table in front of me and looked down on my notes. There was plenty. Chris leaned over to take a peek. "Wow," he exclaimed. "Wow," I answered.

"Thanks my friend," he said. "I truly mean that. This whole idea of us documenting reality was a better experience than I imagined... even if I had to be brutally honest. Even as I might have talked way longer than anyone would want to hear."

"Nothing bad about that…" I moved around the table and grabbed my friend for a hug. He reciprocated nearly lifting me off the ground in a bear hug.

"Did I tell you," he said. "I actually went to a movie by myself. Yeah, I did! It was difficult at first, but not too bad in the end. To be honest with you, I couldn't wait for the lights to go out so no one would see me there alone."

"Was it a love story?" I asked.

He grabbed me around the neck with one arm and gave me a playful noogie. "Nope, it was a pure action flick with all the gunfire and explosions one could imagine. And no viewers in the theater were wrapped in each other's arms in a loving embrace."

"So it was a brain dead movie?"

"Exactly! A high budget, high tech, brain dead, guy movie," he replied.

"I actually went to a concert by myself too."

"Really?" I asked, surprisingly.

"Yeah, I had bought two tickets months earlier; really great seats too. Well, long story short, the person who I thought I was going to go with didn't go and after much personal debate and whole hell of a lot of soul searching, I actually went alone."

"Wow! How did that go for you?" I asked curiously. He cracked me up with his reply.

"Actually, the show was really good. As for the empty seat; I had a place to put my coat!"

We both shared a pretty good laugh at that line.

"I just figured that this is now my life and there are a lot of things that I'm going to have to start doing alone, if I want to do them. I even went out to a restaurant alone while away at one of the boy's tournaments. It was a Chinese restaurant and I still have the little paper from the inside of the fortune cookie I had gotten with the beef and broccoli that I ordered that day. I wrote the date on the back. The fortune read, 'If you're still hungry, have another fortune cookie.' No bullshit. I still have it as a reminder to what my life would be from that day forward. In all honesty, that sucked. Next time you go to a restaurant, take a look around you and see just how many 'solo diners' there are out there. Not too many; that much I can tell you."

We had been through so much during our lengthy conversation. Chris had a huge heart, more than anyone could imagine. He was an honest man. We gathered up and threw our garbage in the trashcan then we walked to our cars and he turned to me and said, "A grandfather one day."

He said, jokingly pointing to his own big frame, "Wow."

"And a great one," I replied.

"Just don't give me the crap about 50 being the new 20."

"I'm not a believer in that one either, especially after hours sitting on these benches."

"Down the road," he said. "Let's double date. Maybe if I seek I will find."

"Anytime, but we are friends so let's get together more often."

He discussed how he now considers his life, at this time to be similar to that of an older rock band making their final concert tour. He asked aloud that while he's in his early now, how much longer is he on this earth. Chris jokingly said the he was "two thirds of the way done" with this life and that he knows the remaining years would almost certainly get harder as the time went on. He described this part of his journey as the "loneliest time." He proudly admitted to me that he wants to try to die with a little dignity. He called this part of his life and the efforts to resurrect something good out of the ills of a divorce as his "Dying with Dignity Tour." We both laughed openly at the comparison but I knew that it hurt him so much more than he was going to show me. Chris talked of making a concerted effort to exercise regularly and try to get in better shape, to see some good concerts and shows and attempt to chip away at the enormous mountain of debt that he has accumulated over the past few years since his separation. He wants to live his life as a participant, not merely just as a spectator. He then solemnly confided in me that his ultimate goal was to continue to never stop trying to mend the fragile relationships that he currently shares with his children. Chris also made a promise to himself; that no matter how difficult times ahead become, he would try to laugh a little each day. He even told me of his ultimate plan to purchase a small home that he could call his own; a place where he can hang his own photos on the walls, mow his own lawn and park his own car in his own driveway.

One of the hardest things for Chris to do from this point forward was to build some resemblance of a legacy to leave for his children; for he knew that time would not be on his side. It bothered me when he said that he feels, deep down inside, that if he didn't wake up tomorrow, everything that he had in the boxes of his small apartment right now would probably just end up in a nearby dumpster. He didn't hold his future in high regard and I have to admit, this was disturbing to me. I guess maybe that Chris had come to a realization that his life will never quite be the way he thought it would be. Not exactly "happily ever after."

Chris hugged me again; though thankfully not as tightly, and then climbed into his SUV. He turned for a moment and smiled that large grin. I half waved and then just like that he was off towards the exit. I pondered a moment hoping that Chris would keep busy. Travel maybe. Continue his photography, definitely. I got into my car and headed for the parks exit.

As of this final draft Chris is still not yet divorced. He does not have that finalization that would allow him his freedom. His wife is still resentful, and I'm sure is still hurting deeply within. He has also slipped in and out of a few passing moments with an occasional companion. Deep down in the depths of Chris' soul, he knows exactly where his happiness lies. It is simply the passing of time, which Chris must endure; the healing of wounds, which have scarred so deeply the people that he loves the most. For it is that passing of the most precious gift of time, which that will eventually bring Chris to his happiest and sacred place;

ultimately allowing him to find his inner peace.

Sadly, this past Christmas was no better than the first after his separation. The boys still collectively choose not to visit his apartment. Chris tried to stay by himself through most of the day. When he finally did visit with his relatives, he kept a phony smile pasted on his face, as he pretended in front of them, that he was in the Holiday Spirit. He went to bed early as well on New Year's Eve. "Amateur Night," he used to call it. Chris has made a resolution to try to socialize more and spend a little more time out with friends. I was overjoyed to hear that; not allowing the loneliness to have the stranglehold on him as it once did.

Before Chris left that day in the park, he stopped his SUV briefly and decided to leave me with a joke. He loved jokes; short and to the point. "Hey, this is the longest that I've ever sat with you and not told you a joke! Are you ready for one?" Although it wasn't my life that we were talking about, I looked at him and said, "Sure, I think we're both ready for a good joke!"

"Ok," he said. "Here it goes...a little girl and a little boy were at day care one day. The girl approaches the boy and says, 'Hey Tommy, do you want to play house?' He says, 'Sure, what do you want me to do?' The little girl replies, 'I want you to communicate your thoughts.' 'Communicate my thoughts?' said the bewildered Tommy. 'I have no idea what that means.' The little girl just smirks and says, 'Perfect. You can be the husband.'"

The Pain & Suffering of Divorce

This chapter focuses on the effects of divorce on the lives of mothers and children of divorce and the pain and suffering they experience. I do not mean to imply that women without children suffer any less intensely when they divorce. We concentrated on the impact of divorce on families because we also wanted to highlight the children's pain and suffering. I will try to outline some of the common feelings and circumstances that occur and relay the stories of two fictional, "composite" women who typify some of the typical experiences that divorced mothers encounter depending on where their children reside. Sally will have residential custody of her children like the vast majority of divorced mothers while Sara will not.

Since the circumstances leading to divorce are different in each case the resulting feelings of anger, resentment, betrayal, alienation, abandonment, failure and loneliness also necessarily differ in magnitude. In addition, no two people feel exactly the same amount of each these emotions because of our individual differences, circumstances, experiences and perceptions. It is always easier for the partner who initiates the divorce to cope with the experience then it is for the partner who receives the life altering news. The partner who initiates the divorce has already begun to "move on emotionally" while the other partner seems to never catch up.

In spite of popular belief, not everyone who wants a divorce has someone else waiting in the wings. The causes of infidelity occur long before any cheating takes place when couples become distant and resentful of each other. This sometimes leads to an emotional affair with a third party and that is how Sara became involved with another man.

Sara was a successful, professional woman who worked long hours and was not home to check homework or make dinner for her two children. Sara's husband Joe who ran a successful business with a flexible work schedule carried out those roles. Joe was consequently more available to the children and was more bonded to them than Sara was. This arrangement allowed a strong mutual resentment to begin between Sara and Joe based on the different roles they played in the family. Sara resented Joe because he got to relax at home with their son and daughter more often and Joe resented Sara because "she was never home." Their mutual resentment eventually spread to other areas of their relationship. Sara was frustrated by Joe's lesser income, necessitating her to work long hours. She also resented Joe's tendency to vent his frustration to the kids who began to view their mom in a very negative light. Joe was upset about the frequent business calls that Sara received at home after hours and on weekends. He began to accuse Sara of rejecting the children in favor of her career. The groundwork for an emotional affair with a coworker whose wife also resented his long hours at work was set.

In spite of popular belief, it is not always the husband who has the extra-marital affair. I have seen many cases where the wife had the affair leading to the divorce. The reasons for pursuing the affairs may differ but wives cheat on their husbands almost as often as husbands' cheat on their wives. The husbands seem to get caught more often because wives are much more careful about their extra-marital affairs. They are also more intuitive and often sense something is going on with their husbands while many husbands' egos do not allow them to believe their wives may be cheating on them.

I have seen cases where the wives were having discrete extra- marital affairs for ten or twenty years without the husbands suspecting anything. The husbands on the other hand usually get caught cheating by their wives within a few months of the affair beginning because they are not as careful. Many wives also know intuitively that their husbands have strayed. Wives may notice that their husbands do not approach them as often for sex, that they are taking extra care of their appearance or they just look guilty.

Sara and Joe gradually stopped making love to each other as their relationship deteriorated further. This weakens the bond between couples and provides a suitable rationale for either partner to become physically involved with someone else. Emotional affairs, which often begin as venting sessions about respective spouses, frequently end up as full-blown affairs when both parties reduce sexually activity with their respective spouses. This was the progression Sara's life took with a handsome, understanding coworker.

Once Sara began having a torrid sexual relationship with her "friend" Sam at work, life evolved quickly for her and every member of her family. Sara fell deeply into infatuation with Sam mistaking it for true love that only develops over time. She began spending even more time away from her family and experienced the romance, passion and happiness that she longed for. She felt validated by Sam and pursued her relationship with him like a high school girl in love for the first time. Sara's new found happiness was evident to every one she knew. Her husband Joe finally realized that something was very wrong and hired a private investigator to follow Sara. Joe found out very quickly that Sara and Sam were a lot more than work friends.

Joe had the process server deliver the divorce papers at work in order to cause Sara the most discomfort. Sara quickly moved into her own apartment and thought it best for her children to remain with their father. Joe was after all the primary care taker of the children. Little did Sara know that this decision would further damage her relationship with her children. She also did not realize that no two marriages implode at the same rate and that Sam was going to try to repair his marriage one more time.

Sara took the news that Sam was not leaving his wife very badly. She was at first shocked and then depressed and tearful about it for weeks. Her depression was compounded when Sara realized that her two children blamed her for the break- up of the family. The children felt abandoned and rejected when Sara moved out of the family home. When her children began refusing to see Sara the pain and emptiness in the pit of her stomach became overwhelming and an antidepressant was added to her counseling regimen to enable Sara to maintain an adequate level of functioning.

The pain Sara had over losing her children emotionally was similar to the grief parents experience losing their children through death. Sara's children continued to reject her in spite of court ordered family counseling and supervised visitation. This sequence of events and the resulting pain is exactly what typically happens to divorced fathers everyday across the country. Fathers almost always are separated from their children if the marriage ends in divorce.

Society routinely ignores the pain that divorced fathers feel being separated from their children but almost every one will judge mothers who leave their children even more harshly. People are aghast to hear of a mother who left her children even if she recognized that the children were better off with their father. Sara did not receive any support from her family and friends when she needed it the most. She had lost her children, Sam and Joe and only found acceptance and empathy during individual and group counseling. Her relationships with her two children were severely damaged and only the passage of time and her children maturing will enable them to heal.

Most children who become estranged from a parent as a result of divorce eventually resume the relationship as they mature into adulthood. For some children of divorce, the resumption of the relationship with the estranged parents begins during college when the young adults are separated from both parents. This gives them the opportunity to develop their own opinions and perspectives independent of either parent. Other adult children resume their relationship with the estranged parent when they plan their weddings or after the birth of their own children. The idea of either parent not being at the wedding or the new born children not knowing a grandparent are powerful motivators to resume a relationship with an estranged parent.

Unfortunately, divorced children often have a pattern of allowing the estranged parent back into their lives temporarily when they want something the residential custodial parent cannot or will not provide. It may be a ride to see a friend at an inconvenient time but is more often a purchase of an item the residential parent is refusing to buy such as new electronic devices or sporting goods equipment.

Estranged parents often become aware they are being used by their children and allow it to continue just to have contact with them or some influence in their lives. However, the closeness they had with their children before divorcing often does not return and adds to the pain and hurt in the pit of the estranged parent's stomach.

The children of divorce may suffer their own heart wrenching pain when their parents announce they are divorcing, when a parent moves out of the family home, when either parent starts a new romantic relationship or has another child. Many children initially go through a grieving process when a parent leaves the home that often evolves into anger and rejection. Most feel that the parent who leaves the home is abandoning them instead of a painful marriage. They also witness the pain, anger and frustration of the parent they reside with toward the parent who leaves the home. Many parents cannot refrain from making negative comments about the other parent to the children. It is also impossible to keep children from overhearing negative comments made to other family members and friends. These negative influences add to the resentment the children feel toward the parent who leaves the home.

By adolescence, children of divorce often begin refusing to see the parent who moved out of the family residence. Most adolescent and teenage children respond poorly to being forced to visit with a parent especially if the visits interrupt their social plans. This often creates even more anger and resentment of the estranged parent.

It is much more common for children of divorce to be estranged from their fathers because mothers are usually given residential custody of the children unless the mother has a history of psychiatric illness, drug or alcohol treatments or criminal activity. Since the standard court ordered visitation is usually every other weekend and one or two nights during the week, the mother carries out the majority of parenting responsibilities. This was the circumstance with Sally who had residential custody of her three children.

Sally had been divorced for two years when she began receiving counseling to manage her stress and treat her depression. She had returned to her job as a secretary and worked part time but she was a full-time parent and homemaker to her daughter and two sons. Sally was chronically on the run trying her best to meet all of her children's needs and provide them with every opportunity life had to offer. There were three sets of everything including but not limited to doctor and dentist appointments, sporting events and practices, parent-teacher conferences, religious instruction and socializing with friends. Sally had no time for herself and no time for a relationship. She was depressed, angry and overwhelmed about her circumstances and resentful of her former husband Ron.

Sally believed that Ron had the life because he had few of the parenting responsibilities she had. Ron was a teacher who would have loved to spend more time with his children if he didn't need a second job to pay his bills and child support. He struggled to survive financially, living in a basement apartment that he found depressing and embarrassing. Ron was forced to leave the beautiful home that he and Sally recently remodeled. He was extremely resentful of Sally who will be able to maintain the comfortable life style they both had enjoyed together until her youngest son finishes college. All courtesy of an archaic court system designed when men went to work to support their families while women stayed home to run the household and take care of the family and children played every day with neighborhood friends.

This arrangement may have been suitable in the 1950's or 60's but certainly is not viable for most present day American families. The current system of giving residential custody to one parent while requiring the other to "visit" with the children and pay child support damages the lives and relationships of every member of the family but especially the children, the very people the courts are trying to protect.

American divorce courts try to make sure a stable home environment and financial support are provided for the children after their parents' divorce. It is supposed to ensure that noncustodial parents pay their fair share of child support and that they continue to have "contact" with their children. However, all of us know divorced women who do not receive adequate child support needed to feed, clothe and house their children. Many divorced fathers play a shell game with their finances, often working off the books to avoid paying their fair share of taxes and child support. I have seen countless divorced fathers drive into my office parking lot with expensive luxury cars while paying their ex-wives a small fraction of what they should be paying in child support. Likewise, I have seen countless divorced fathers who are distraught about not seeing their children enough or at all.

The standard visitation of every other weekend and one or two nights during the week is enough to maybe be an uncle or an aunt but not an involved, loving parent. Many children of divorce lose their emotional bond with their fathers and develop intense anger and resentment toward him and either severely limit their contact or refuse to see their fathers at all. The anger and resentment increases exponentially if the father tries to parent by imposing limits or consequences. This was the case with Sally and Ron's three children.

Ron's 17-year-old son Jason and his 12-year-old daughter Rachel had been refusing to see him at all when I met both of them two years after their parents divorced. Their 15-year-old brother Patrick occasionally saw their father but he only did so when he wanted something from Ron. The family was court ordered to receive counseling in a third attempt to restore normal relationships between the children and their father. The stress of this long, expensive legal battle within the family was taking its' toll on each of them.

Every member of the family was angry and upset and experiencing some form of emotional distress including disturbed sleep, upset stomachs, poor concentration at work or school and panic attacks. The three children were angry about being forced to attend weekly family counseling sessions and were unreceptive to therapeutic techniques to reduce excessive negative emotion or to give a relationship with their father another try. They blamed Ron for all the turmoil in their lives and they saw every attempt he made to see them as an intrusion in their lives.

Ron reported to me that his relationship with his three children began deteriorating shortly after he left the house. His relationship with Sally continued to be mutually hostile and antagonistic after the divorce as so often is the case with couples that divorce under the current settlement procedures. Ron blamed Sally for the poor relationships he had with each of his three children. He accused Sally of totally disregarding the routine divorce stipulation to not speak disparagingly about the other parent. Sally insisted his visitation with the children follow the stipulation in the divorce agreement, every other weekend and one night during the week. The bond between Ron and each of his children were broken and he knew it. His heart ached for the company of his children and he looked forward to each visit with them but Ron was always disappointed with the outcome.

The children would usually arrive late, leave early or have an activity that conflicted with the visitation. Ron began to feel that Sally was purposely scheduling their activities during his visitation but in speaking with Sally I knew it was impossible to avoid these conflicts with the scheduling demands of today's children. The tension, pain and suffering in their family were about to worsen.

Ron's lawyer began sending threatening letters to Sally about problems with the visitation and after being divorced for two years, Sally and Ron went back to family court. The children blamed Ron for their court ordered counseling, their court appointed attorney and for all the tension and resentment in the family. Their weekly family counseling sessions were insufficient to deal with the magnitude of problems that needed to be addressed and soon failed as it had two previous times.

In my thirty years of private practice I have unfortunately seen too many cases like Ron and Sally's where every member of the family and every relationship within it is damaged by giving residential custody to one parent while requiring the other parent to "visit" the children and pay child support. While not every divorced family is as damaged as Ron and Sally's family and wind up in court ordered counseling, the majority of divorced families are experiencing some level of psychological distress and damage to the relationship between the children and the visiting parent. The effects of the psychological distress and damage to the parent child relationship can have a negative impact on children for the rest of their lives.

I have treated countless adults from divorced families who have problems relating to others, even their own children, as a result of a poor or nonexistent relationship with an estranged parent. Damage to the bond between the child and the estranged parent often has lifelong impact on how we relate to others as adults. The consequences of divorce and the pain and suffering it causes every family member but especially the children, may all be avoided if some flexibility and common sense changes are built into the divorce process. The next chapter will outline some practical changes to the divorce settlements that would help minimize the pain and suffering and dysfunction caused by divorce.

The two previous chapters focused on the pain and suffering of divorce and the damage to the parent- child relationship caused by giving residential custody to one parent while requiring the other parent to "visit" with his or her children. The current chapter will present some common sense recommendations that are designed to minimize the psychological impact of divorce on every member of the family but especially the children.

Since this chapter is written by a practicing psychologist who treats children, parents and families, it should come as no surprise to the reader that I strongly recommend family counseling before, during and after the divorce with a licensed psychologist or social worker in cases involving minor children. There are several important factors that can be addressed in family counseling that would reduce the psychological distress on family members and avoid potential harm to the relationships between children and parents.

First and foremost, parents must be made aware of the importance of the parent- child bond and ensure that it is maintained with both parents during and after the divorce. The parent- child bond is established and maintained through frequent contact with family members who live and eat together, support each other and engage in family activities together.

The bond provides children with a foundation of security, allows parents to have an influence in their children's lives and promotes a feeling of belonging between the parent and child. It also helps develop relationship skills and comfort relating to male and female adults both critical to the future psychological health of the child. The bond cannot be established or maintained with a visitation schedule of every other weekend and one or two nights during the week whether the parents are married or divorced. Once the bond is broken it becomes impossible to parent a child. The parent becomes marginalized in the child's life. Children refuse to accept parental limits or boundaries from a parent when the bond is broken.

I have unfortunately treated children from intact families every week for over thirty years who do not have an emotional bond with one of their parents. This may be the result of an absent parent, a parent's work schedule or work related travel, or an inability of the parent to bond with his or her child due to the parent's emotional problems or immaturity. It is very confusing to the child and disturbing to me as a psychologist, when a parent tries to establish an emotional bond with his or her child(ren) during the divorce process in order to win residential custody and avoid paying the other parent child support. The degree of bond between the child(ren) and each parent is a critical factor in deciding residential custody and it should be assessed by forensic psychologists who are specially trained to make these assessments. When both parents have established bonds with their children it is extremely important that residential custody agreements safeguard those bonds.

Split or joint residential custody where children alternate residency with both parents is the best way to preserve the parent- child bond with each parent. I have seen parents, split days or weeks in order to provide their children with maximal time with both parents. Some families alternate weeks with the absent parent being given visitation during their off week. These kinds of arrangements ensure that one parent will not be over burdened with parenting responsibilities while the other parent only assumes parental obligations during visitation. It allows both parents time to reestablish their lives and to develop new and hopefully healthier romantic relationships. There are other important benefits to split residential custody.

Split residential custody can eliminate the need for child support when both parents are able to work, and provide adequate supervision of the children. Each parent would be financially responsible for the child(ren) during the time spent with that parent. This would provide parents with a financial incentive to directly care for and supervise their children to avoid childcare costs. An increase in direct parental supervision has obvious benefits over child care. The elimination of child support and reimbursement for child care when possible would reduce hostility between parents and foster better working relationships. The reduction in hostility between parents would benefit the child(ren) by reducing the tension and stress in the family and the tendency of parents to bad mouth each other to the child(ren). Negative comments by one parent against the other are damaging to the parent- child relationship.

The tendency for a divorced parent to speak disparagingly about the other parent in front of their children is unfortunately quite common in spite of divorce stipulations to the contrary. This tendency creates considerable stress for children, making it more difficult for them to cope with their parents' divorce and to remain bonded to both parents. The topic can be addressed and monitored in family counseling with parents and children before, during and after the divorce. Other topics of family counseling that would foster improved psychological health for children of divorce are outlined below.

The importance of having agreed upon parental rules,

expectations and limits cannot be over emphasized. Parental agreement in these areas reduces the children's hostility toward a stricter parent, reduces acting out behavior and increases the children's cooperation with both parents. It also reduces the tendency of some parents to compete for their children's affection by showering them with gifts or privileges. Proactive family counseling can also reduce the tendencies of children to manipulate parents or to pit one parent against the other to maximize gain. The goal of family counseling in the divorce process is to protect the psychological health of the child and to improve or maintain the parent-child bond.

The critical component in establishing or maintaining the parent-bond is frequent contact between the child and the parent. A parent or court order should not limit contact unless one parent is clearly emotionally handicapped as indicated by repeated inpatient treatment for a psychiatric condition or drug and alcohol abuse. Both parents should want to facilitate contact with the other parent to foster the psychological health and development of the child. A parent who discourages contact with the other parent in the absence of a clearly established psychological disturbance is not acting in the best interest of the child.

One would have to question the intentions of a parent that discourages contact between their children and their other parent. All of us have met parents that are overly involved in their children's lives. Some divorced parents continue fighting with or punishing their former spouses through their children. Other parents wage a battle of influence in the lives of their children. Each of these circumstances are damaging to the psychological health of the child and the parent child- bond. Parents should be cooperating with each other to ensure that children are getting enough contact with each parent to maintain a healthy bond. Children thrive when both parents are actively involved in their lives. Involvement can be increased in a variety of ways whether parents are married or divorced.

Parents who do not have residential custody can offer the parent who does, help with childcare and transportation to school, sports and other activities. It can be extremely difficult for one parent to provide all the transportation needs for children especially in large families or when children participate in multiple activities. Parental attendance at activities also shows children they are supported and are a priority in their parents' lives. Some parents share an interest with their children and volunteer their time to become team coaches.

This can significantly increase the amount of time spent together and improve the parent child bond.

Finally, it is recommended that parents live close enough to their children to allow them the opportunity to informally visit while riding their bikes or moving around the neighborhood. It greatly increases children's security and confidence knowing that both parents are nearby and available to them. While it may be difficult at first for divorced parents to live in the same town, the psychological advantages to the child greatly outweigh any discomfort experienced by the parents.

Coping with Divorce

The authors of this manuscript have done their best to illustrate the pain and suffering of divorce on adults and children in previous chapters. Recommendations for some common sense changes in American divorce courts that would reduce the suffering of children and parents were also offered. This chapter will assist the reader in finding support to cope with divorce and accessing counseling from licensed mental health specialists. A list of suggested readings and websites concludes the chapter.

Many suffer silently through the divorce process without sharing it with close friends or family to avoid personal embarrassment. Some may be fearful of disapproval from members of their support system. Others may view themselves as failures instead of victims of failed marriages and may choose to hide their pain and suffering from everyone in their life. Sharing news of an impending divorce with friends and loved ones can be a significant step in the process for many of us. While care must be taken in deciding who to initially share this information with, it can be extremely comforting to share your pain and suffering with supportive friends and family. Many of us however require more support and comfort than our loved ones can possibly provide.

It is strongly recommended that counseling be sought from only licensed psychologists and social workers who have experience treating adults and children of divorce. The reader is cautioned to avoid treatment from unlicensed counselors who may refer to themselves as "psychotherapists." Licensed psychologist and social workers that specialize in divorce can provide the support and coping strategies required to deal with the divorce. Most health insurers reimburse for medically necessary psychological treatments from licensed psychologists and social workers. Support groups, family counseling and individual counseling are available to assist adults and children through the divorce process. Referrals to skilled mental health specialists often come from health insurance companies, primary care physicians, friends and family who have good experiences with practitioners and local professional organizations such as county psychological associations. Many public school systems provide support groups like the Banana Splits program to help children cope with their parents' divorce. These support group programs are led by school psychologists and social workers who can also assist families in accessing treatment.

Experienced, licensed mental health specialists recognize when psychotropic medication may be necessary and make appropriate referrals to psychiatrists or primary care physicians. Psychotropic medications to reduce chronic emotional upset, depression or anxiety are sometimes required in order to enable some adults to keep functioning during the divorce process. If you are unable to sleep, stop crying, or you are constantly upset and unable to work or get through your daily routine, a physician should determine if psychotropic medication may be an appropriate treatment to help reduce suffering and improve functioning.

Psychiatrists specialize in prescribing appropriate psychoactive medications to help control debilitating levels of chronic emotional upset, depression and anxiety. In many parts of the country however, it is extremely difficult to get an appointment with a psychiatrist due to shortages of psychiatrists. Primary care physicians are often willing to write prescriptions for commonly prescribed psychoactive medications but may not be comfortable prescribing uncommon or multiple psychotropic medications. Psychiatric Nurse Practitioners are also trained to prescribe psychotropic medications and have been filling the shortage of psychiatrists in some areas of the country. While children may have initial emotional upset upon first hearing about their parents' divorce, it is very rare that they become unable to function. Children may manifest the stress of their parent's divorce through lower academic performance or increased defiance but they are usually still able to get out of bed and go to school. However, as discussed in previous chapters, the effects of divorce on children can be more insidious and long term and family counseling is strongly recommended when children are involved. Family counseling can help to protect the parent child-bond, which is critical to a child's emotional development. It can also help divorcing parents proactively avoid some of the circumstances that contribute to future problems like children rejecting parenting from the visiting parent. As discussed in previous chapters, parents often compete for influence over the children by providing unearned gifts and privileges to them. Insufficient time with the visiting parent coupled with unearned gifts and privileges may result in increased behavioral and emotional difficulties in children.

While "self - help books" to cope with divorce are often very useful adjuncts, they are not substitutes for counseling from mental health specialists or sharing pain and suffering with supportive friends, family and others who may also be experiencing the gut wrenching effects of divorce. A list of suggested readings and websites follows to assist adults and children in coping with divorce but they do not replace the healing that occurs when people help and support each other through difficult times.

On Closure...

Before publication the authors agreed that there was still one lingering question. What about closure? Michael and Chris are left with confusion and doubt pertaining to their futures. There exists no empathy in their relationship with their ex-spouses and children. It was the authors' hope that forgiveness would be a fundamental ingredient of closure and we encouraged it in numerous interviews.

My phone calls with Michael were as such:

"I was stunned," Michael told me. "My therapist agreed with you Vince. He suggested I bring my ex-wife in with the children and we all try to talk."

"Not such a bad idea," I said.

I could almost see him shaking his head. "I told him it wouldn't work. She would emphatically contradict every word I ever said."

"Mike, there wasn't any damage that couldn't be repaired, as far as I could see. Arguing over the kids and about money. No serious betrayal and even if there were..."

"Funny, that's what he said. Dr. V told me to let him try and deal with any negatives that came from my ex... He told me it would be a major positive for the kids, for anyone's kids, at any age. And his hope was that the bickering was over, or at least taken down a few notches."

"I like Dr. V," I said.

"Ha, ha," Michael laughed. "Bring in the enemy. The one who humiliated me by shutting me out of everything and any decisions that needed to be made in regards to my kids...The one who wanted me broke and dragged into court while she splurged and spoiled herself and the children with lavish shopping and vacations."

"Mike, we spoke at length about the reality; it is more than possible she was hurting as much as you were."

"For all I know I was a cuckold. I know I became the orphaned parent. The parent from a broken home."

"I'm interested in what Dr. V had to say." I could hear Mike breathe. With the cell phone on speaker I'm certain he was pacing, eager to once again vent a number of specifics I already knew about, plus some.

"Vin you know how many times since I've been single I've made a drunken fool of myself trying to talk to women?"

"And that's your ex-wife's fault how?" Michael didn't answer instead continued on about his therapist. "He thinks our conflicts are somewhat repairable and shouldn't last a lifetime. He knows my children, he says they love me and he believes them when they tell him their mother does not want to be my enemy..."

"I think he is right Mike. I really do. But I'm not going to push. Whatever damage there is, it's now done with. Maybe she needs to forgive you too."

"Forgive me?" he stated. "What a joke. I'm the one on the outside looking in, walking on eggshells. I'm afraid all the time that I might say the wrong thing. That I will oppose their mother's views, especially the ones that are beneficially spoiling them. They will only alienate me more! I can't parent because she's their best friend."

Luckily the road to healing for Michael did not hinge on just my suggestions, although ironically I was in agreement with the views of his therapist. Dr. V, his presumed ally, was guiding him, I believe, in the right direction. Michael had been disclosing his frustrations for a very long time, his trials and tribulations. He was honest about his faults his anger and disappointments. But it still was just one side.

Dr. V's intentions were not to get the pair into a room and fight a cage match, but to navigate them towards a peace. He assumed with the passage of time two rational people could see clear to understand each other and filter much of the anger. "It just might work," he told Michael. And yes; for the children's sake.

I tossed my theory at him. "As time passes there really can be a healing process. Old wounds though not forgotten can begin to close." Michael was reluctant.

"Forgiveness is a religious concept Vin.

"Hard to wrap my head around the idea of forgiving someone who basically couldn't give a fuck if I dropped dead."

"You don't know---"

"Yes, yes, I know what you're going to say. But let's face it the concept of forgiving without forgetting is an oxymoron. If you can't forget how the hell do you let go?"

"I think Dr. V knows what he's talking about. Stick with him and let him guide you through this in a professional manner."

Dr. V explained to Mike the children's perspectives. All

they see are their parents at odds. It is very uncomfortable for them and they find it difficult to intercede. Dr. V clarified the enormity of forgiveness and he told Mike not be combative, that he would fairly and professionally intercede when Michael and his ex would turn any conversation into an ugly confrontation. The old adage 'we agree to disagree,' will now certainly apply.

"Your kids say, and agree, that their mom would very much like to join us in a session," Dr. V told Michael.

"How does that happen doc? I can't call her and I haven't text or emailed her in forever."

"Well you're going to have to make the first move. I suggest a polite e-mail."

"What if she says no?"

"If she says no, then it is no. But you will then be relieved of any doubt. And be mindful, to be humble is to realize right off the bat that she might not warm to your idea, and that means if she doesn't, under any circumstances do you then attack...Bitterness my friend can last many years, too many. Forgiveness can begin to lift the cloud."

Michael reminded Dr. V of the struggles to see eye to eye with his ex and the good Dr. responded: "If you're going to do this you must stop picking out only the things that drove you insane or still do...And more importantly if you decide not to reach out to your ex then you have to work on letting go and take what time will bring. You will have to stop wondering about the, what if's, and stick by your decision. I of course will help you through it."

As Michael's friend, I could say I liked this doctor.

Michael reiterated the difficulty in reaching out to his ex. What would he say? Would she answer? Would she answer sarcastically? But Dr. V was right. It was Michael, not the children, not the Dr., who must invite the ex-wife into the new conversation. The only thing I could offer my friend was to remind him to toss out the pride. Suck it up. Yes, do it for the children, for the rest of your family. I encouraged him to remember a line he stated from a previous interview, "No resolution is haunting."

Michael could be defiant and a tense anger could push to the forefront with the mere mention of his ex-wife. However, he loved his children and intellectually he knew the only way to sooth old wounds was to somehow make amends with her.

Michael had to humble himself and keep in mind the mean verbal assault he had once spewed to his ex to try and diminish her. Hold back the blame. I could remind him a thousand times but somehow a person gets it more when he's paying for an opinion.

"Yes, yes," Dr. V had agreed. "We know you feel left behind, we know you feel disrespected, yes..." But Dr. V reiterated to him of his admitted shortcomings. He told Michael he didn't have to obsess and cast all the blame on himself but to simply remember his emotional and physical laziness during his marriage. Not always intentional he left his wife to carry much of the decisions along with most of the household chores. Mike inhaled a newly lit cigarette. "Vince, I remember the smiles on their sweet faces before the property issues took center stage in a courtroom where the presumed love of my life had morphed into a complete stranger. Before all that when I picked the kids up for Thanksgiving and Christmas I would leave my ex-wife with a kiss and warm wishes for the holiday. Those faces were confused but smiling nevertheless."

"Balance it," I told him "Again you are concentrating on the emotions that get YOU upset."

I sensed he heard what I was attempting to explain but as if stuck in reverse he continued. "Suddenly, the kids, as if they missed something in a flash through a winter slumber, mom and dad no longer talked..."

Michael breathed an exaggerated sigh. I knew he was tired of the entire negative pressure he had been letting engulf his mind. He was guilty in some way because his kids lived with the hope that their parents might at least dance again someday. But what I really liked about Mike was his artistic soul and I knew his fervent nature could change his course of thinking on a dime.

From Michael's account Dr. V was a bald, semi-bear of a man, with wire framed glasses and a graying goatee. He was a man with a strong handshake, yet a man who exuded caring smiles, who could laugh with a true heart and loved all the arts. So I pictured the good doctor reminding Michael of his own sense of artistry. I could see Dr. V squinting and gingerly pointing a chubby finger at Mike to remind him of his admitted foibles. "Remember my friend your own admissions of laziness in your marriage. I know you're not malicious but again many times too lazy to help your wife with many of the physical chores, and of course too lazy to iron out or explain or discuss emotional tantrums. Those moments where you truly had no feeling of contrition." And I could visualize Michael tut-tutting, looking for a cigarette, and squinting his sharp blue eyes as the doctor brought home Michael's penchant for the novel.

"In how many books my friend, or even movies, have you realized that when a man feels pain he becomes stupid."

"I remembered Dr. V's sessions about my own garbage and coincidently as I was obsessing in my car one day I heard a Sinatra gem on the radio. A song I hadn't heard before, 'I Believe I'm Gonna Love You.' Michael seemed to be pushed along with the magic of lyrics and strings in a song. "Vin, I heard this song on the radio. Just when I thought I heard everything from Frank here hits me this hidden treasure. It nearly brought me to tears."

I don't know how many cigarettes Michael smoked during our phone sessions but he bursts out short puffs more frequently.

"I thought seriously of what Dr. V had said. 'Michael, you're a lover of art. Make the story work for you.'"

And so, like a blocked writer trying to find the words for a difficult chapter, Michael, nervous I'm sure, sat poised in front of the computer screen. So, remembering his ex-wife's last e-mail, almost a year earlier, one that he rejected, before all hell broke loose, where she stated the story of their children, the many memories and life events that needed to be shared. Her desire not to let their anger get in the way...

Dear....

How Do We Heal?

While conducting the numerous interviews which comprise the content of this manuscript, the authors observed a common thread at the end of each exhaustive interview process; the desire for the participants to somehow find healing and closure in their now shattered worlds. We cannot describe the pain on people's faces, men and women alike who, once we've scrapped it all down to bare metal, have expressed a desire to somehow find solace within their lives. Separation/divorce is no small matter. Be it amicable or not, the feelings of resentment, of failure, of loss and of helplessness continue to fill our souls for many, many years to follow.

Many would argue that it could also be considered to be a traumatic incident; and why not? You meet a partner, you fall in love, you get married, you buy a house, you raise a family and eventually, you rest on the security that all that you have put into this life will allow you to sit back in your latter years and enjoy the fruits of your labor. All the time that you've invested in each other, in your children, in your lives together as a family, all of a sudden comes to a screeching halt.

Your partner is gone, he or she no longer shares your dreams, will no longer walk with you, will not be there to enjoy your future. Make no doubt about it; this is a devastating blow. Mental health professionals have at times, equated it with the death of a spouse. How your perfect world, as you have known it, can become a pile of ruin almost overnight, is indeed, a tremendous emotional and psychological loss.

Many of our participants have expressed feeling anxiety when faced with this dilemma. The feeling of an overwhelming life change in such a sudden fashion can feel like an express train leaving the tracks at a very high speed and coming to rest in a ditch on the side of a dark road in the middle of the night. The faint cries you hear from that wreckage are the same cries that you find yourself making when you are alone or late at night, coming from behind your child's bedroom door. Loss, in any form, invokes pain. Pain, in any form, invokes emotion. Emotion, in a negative form, evokes fear. Fear, if even for a short period of time, evokes helplessness. And so the cycle begins.

How do we heal? Therapy is always a smart approach. The thoughts expressed and coping mechanisms learned can lead one to the start of a journey of healing. Therapy takes time. Emotions affect you on a 24-hour basis and a visit to a therapist will only last 45 minutes every week. Add in a doctor's appointment, a sick child or a scheduling conflict and you're bottling up your feelings for two weeks or sometimes longer. That is difficult. Although the benefits of professional therapy are numerous, having a forum to discuss your feelings for a relatively short period of time based on someone else's availability can greatly prolong your proverbial road to recovery.

Then there are friends. Depending on their experiences, their views can be either too radical; "Fuck Him, he screwed you! You're better off without him!" Or they can be too soft and overly optimistic; "It's OK, give it some time and you guys can work this out. You know what they say, 'Love conquers all'…"

Some have elicited the comfort of support groups, which

can encompass many different points of view and help one find healing to some, if not all, of their hurt feelings. Healing can be hard. A Chinese proverb reads, "A journey of a thousand miles begins with one step." Finding the strength to actually take that step and to continue to move forward every single day of your life is most difficult. These are your Dark Days; your weakest moments. These are the times when you feel so alone and your mind just seems to never stop reminding you of your situation. These occur when you're at work, when you're driving a car, when you're at your child's parent/teacher night. They happen so often, that they literally consume your day. How many times have you forgotten where you were going, drove right past your exit or the store that you wanted to go to? How many times have you forgotten an appointment, forgotten to return a phone call or simply found yourself simply crying for no apparent reason? These are the times where one becomes so lonely that it physically hurts. It becomes a pit in your stomach. These are the Dark Days. Time alone can be one's worst enemy. Your heart will tell your mind what it wants to hear and that ray of hope that you cling to so gingerly, continuously lead to yet another disappointment. I'm sure that we have all heard the term, "What a fool believes, he sees." Truer words have never been spoken when you are surviving through a Dark Day.

A kind word or gesture from an ex-partner subconsciously gives a sense of hope that will, without question, impose upon you more rejection and more pain. You may take small steps forward but getting knocked down like that yet again, will send you back a long, long way. Sometimes our instincts force us to see the good in everyone, but sometimes, you should be cautioned, not everyone has goodness within them. Emotional pain that is so intense will long for anything that may lead it to some simple form of relief. Have you ever watered a plant whose flowers were wilting; its color brown. Lay the hose above that plant for a few moments and let the water take deep into its roots. You will undoubtedly see this plant and its beautiful flowers, blossom again. Deep inside, we all want to be those flowers; simply coming back to life with the simple flowing of life enabling water. Our broken hearts yearn for that water, but unfortunately, this is not always meant to be.

Healing must start from within. For your hurt, anguish and deep seeded sorrow must be tackled at its core. Finding peace must start from within.

Each day must start as a truly new day; leaving no tears or disappointments carried over from the days, weeks or months past. This all must change.

You must wake up every day with a new, fresh and bolder look; a positive but cautious sense of purpose; an understanding that today will be better than yesterday, but not as good as tomorrow. You need to look in the mirror, and say to yourself, today, I will be stronger. Today, I will be happier. Today, I will take a few more precious steps towards my overall recovery and healing. This is a very difficult task; but one which you already possess the skills to master. Some of us turn to faith. The power of prayer should never be underestimated and one who seeks a spiritual path to healing a damaged soul usually finds their happiness in a truer and more complete form.

One of the many components of faith based healing is forgiveness. Not only forgiveness for the one that has caused you pain, but forgiveness for yourself. Many organized religions incorporate forgiveness in their scripture and it has been constantly spoken of by the likes of Mahatma Gandhi, Martin Luther King and others who have dealt with hurt, persecution and oppression; not only upon themselves, but that which is placed upon many people at the same time. Forgiveness promotes a healing aura, a healing message, a healing culture. When applied correctly, forgiveness goes to one's inner being and cleanses hate, quells resentment and frees us from the burdens of animosity which we so deeply hold. It has been said that we need to forgive to release ourselves from the chains of resentment and retaliation.

The wrong that a person has done to another may never be changed, but it can be forgiven. The first step of forgiveness is willing to forgive. It takes a strong person to say that they are sorry. But it takes a stronger person to forgive. Forgiveness is not only a word; it is an emotion, an absolute feeling. You will feel its enlightening effects the minute that those words leave your mouth. Forgiveness is therapy like no other. Its application is so profound, and comes from so deep within that one cannot help to feel relieved once it is passed along. Forgiveness frees you of hate, resentment and animosity and it allows you to take back control of your life, both emotionally as well as spiritually. One will see, when they assess their situation, that if they are ready to forgive, then they eventually will. If a person has not arrived at that juncture in their lives, then they will go on and continue about their ways, never reaping the benefits of sharing their forgiveness with ones who have hurt them. Forgiveness is not only a gift that you give to yourself; it is truly a gift which you give to another.

When a person has hurt another, especially a spouse, parent or a child, they do eventually look back at their indiscretion and wonder if they could have gone about things entirely different. This is more often the case than not. Having caused hurt to a loved one is not something that one can easily hide from; for the negative feelings within will eventually lead to a desire to make it right and somewhat whole again. However, the reality is that those who caused the hurt usually has to await forgiveness from those which they hurt. This may take years, if it even comes at all. The person who has done the most damage is the person who craves the repentant virtues that forgiveness brings. The person who has caused the pain to another or others is stuck behind the damage and consequences of their actions until their victim(s) decides to forgive them. You would be surprised to learn that most individuals who cause such pain to their loved ones do, over time, desire the forgiveness of those whom they have hurt.

When you choose to forgive those who have hurt you, you actually take away *their* power. By instilling forgiveness upon them, you release yourself from the emotional control that they have over *you*. Forgiveness produces a scenario where all involved are the better for it. *Forgiveness is not and should never be considered as weakness.*

So back to the question, how do we heal? Before anything else, you must first possess a desire to heal. Then you must be ready to forgive.

Suggested Readings:

Moving Forward After Divorce:
Practical Steps to Healing Your Hurts:
Finding Fresh Perspective and Managing Your New Life
David Frisbie, Harvest House, 2006.

Chicken Soup for the Soul: Divorce and Recovery
Jack Canfield, Mark Victor Hansen and Patty Hansen,
Simon & Schuster, 2008.

The Good Divorce by Constance Ahrons
Harper Collins, 1994.

Co-Parenting 101 by Deesh Philyaw and Michael Thomas
New Harbinger Publications, 2013.

How to Talk to Your Children about Divorce: Understanding
What Children May Think, Feel and Need
Jill Jones-Soderman and Allison Quatrocchi, AZ, 2006.

The Truth about Children and Divorce: Dealing with the
Emotions So That You and Your Children Can Thrive
Robert E. Emery, Plume, New York, 2006.

Putting Children First:
Strategies for Helping Children Thrive Through Divorce
Joann Pedro-Carrol, New York Penguin, 2010.

Good Parenting through Divorce: The Essential Guidebook
to Helping Children Adjust and Thrive
Based on The Mary Ellen Hannibal, Dacapopress, 2007.

Helpful Websites:

www.kidsbc.ca

www.kidshealth.org/kid/feeling/home family /divorce.html

www.pbskids.org/itsmylife/family/divorce/index.html.

www.kidshealth.org

www.kidsturncentral.com/topics/issues/divorce.html.

Finding Comfort,
Finding Peace...

While conducting the countless interviews with the men and women who forged the foundation of this manuscript, there came a time that the sessions finally concluded. At that time, immediately following an exhaustive pause, we made it a point to ask our participants what thoughts, quotes or phrases did they read, hear or were shared by someone which afforded them an opportunity to find a sense of comfort during their most difficult days. Many of our respondents were willing to share their favorite quotes with us in an effort to help others find their solace when they needed to fill the voids left from a broken relationship. These are their words. We ask that you too, on your darkest days, turn to the following thoughts and quotes to find your own comfort, peace and strength to get you through to a better tomorrow. Our hope is that in time, you will embrace the infinite wisdom of an old African Proverb - ***"However long the night, the dawn will break."***

"The power in all relationships lies with whoever cares less." ~ Michael Douglas from the movie, *"Ghosts of Girlfriends Past"*

"We must be willing to let go of the life we planned so as to have the life that is waiting for us."
~ Joseph Campbell

"Time decides who you meet in life, your heart decides who you want in your life, and your behavior decides who stays in your life."
~ Ziad K. Abdelnour

"Live life with no regrets. Laugh at the confusion. Smile through the tears and keep reminding yourself that everything happens for a reason."
~ Unknown

"In your lifetime, you will find and meet one person who will love you more than anyone you have ever known and will know. They will love you with every bit of energy and soul. They will sacrifice, surrender and give so much that it scares you. Someday you'll know who that is. Sometimes people realize who it was."
~ Unknown

"As we grow up, we learn that even the one person that wasn't supposed to ever let you down probably will. You will have your heart broken probably more than once and it's harder every time. You'll break hearts too, so remember how it felt when yours was broken. You'll fight with your best friend. You'll blame a new love for things an old one did. You'll cry because time is passing too fast, and you'll eventually lose someone you love. So take too many pictures, laugh too much, and love like you've never been hurt because every sixty seconds you spend upset is a minute of happiness you'll never get back."
~Unknown

"Keep looking up. That's the secret to life."
~Snoopy

"Even on my weakest days, I get a little bit stronger."
~Sara Evans from the song "Stronger"

"Life isn't always a fairytale, that's why you should enjoy the moments when it feels like it is."
~Unknown

"Some of the greatest things in life are unseen. That's why you close your eyes to kiss, cry, or dream."
~Unknown

"Accept what is, let go of what was, have faith in what will be."
~Sonia Ricotti

"It is in your moments of decision that your destiny is shaped."
~Anthony Robbins

"Nobody can go back and start a new beginning, but anyone can start today and make a new ending."
~Maria Robinson

"You may not always end up where you thought you were going, but you will always end up where you were meant to be."
~Unknown

"I'm thankful for my struggle because without it I wouldn't have stumbled across my strength."
~Alex Elle

"Life is too short, grudges are a waste of perfect happiness, laugh when you can, apologize when you should, and let go of what you can't change. Love deeply, and forgive quickly, take chances, give everything, and have no regrets. Life is too short to be unhappy. You have to take the good with the bad, smile when you're sad, love what you've got, and always remember what you had. Always forgive, but never forget, learn from your mistakes, but never regret. People change and things go wrong, but always remember, life goes on."
~Unknown

"You will know you made the right decision when you pick the hardest and most painful choice but your heart is at peace."
~Sabina Tabakovic

"It's useless to hold a person to anything they say when they are in love, drunk, or running for office."
~Shirley MacLaine

"No one looks back on their life and remembers the nights they got plenty of sleep."
~Unknown

"A girl should have two things; a smile and a guy who inspires it."
~Unknown

"Girls want a guy who says I love you every night and proves it every day."
~Unknown

"Distance never separates two people truly in love."
~Unknown

"Distance can't stop what's meant to be."
~Unknown

"Acting in anger never helps. As time passes, the reason for your anger will fade but the things you do in anger stay with you forever as regrets."
~Unknown

"Pain is inevitable. Suffering is optional."
~M. Kathleen Casey

"Just know that wherever you are, I miss you and wish that you were here."
~Unknown

"Whatever you do, hold on to hope! The tiniest thread will twist into an unbreakable cord. Let hope anchor you in the possibility that this is NOT the end of your story; that change will bring you to peaceful shores."
~Unknown

"Love who your heart wants, not what your eyes want. Don't worry what others think. This is your love, not theirs."
~Anonymous

"Anyone can catch your eye but it takes someone special to capture your heart."
~Unknown

"Hurting back the people who hurt you makes you just like them."
~Unknown

"Good relationships don't just happen. They take patience and two people who truly want to be together."
~Unknown

"A silent hug means 1000 words to an unhappy heart."
~Kemmy Nola

"One day they'll realize they lost a diamond while playing with worthless stones."
~Turcois Ominek

"Choose your life's mate carefully. From this decision will come 90% of all your happiness or misery."
~H. Jackson Brown Jr.

"One of the hardest decisions you will ever face in life is choosing whether to walk away or try harder."
~Ziad K. Abdelnour

"True love is when you love someone till your last breath."
~Brigitte Nicole

"When you meet the right person, you know it. You can't stop thinking about them. They are your best friend and your soul mate. You can't wait to spend the rest of your life with them. No one and nothing else can compare."
~Quote from "How I Met Your Mother" sitcom

"When two people really care about each other, they will always look for a way to make it work. No matter how hard it is."
~Unknown

"Love is not who you can see yourself with; it is who you can't see yourself without."
~Jared Leto

"It's sweet when someone remembers every detail about you. Not because you reminded them, but because they pay attention to you."
~Unknown

"Life should not be a journey to the grave with the intention of arriving safely in a pretty and well preserved body, but rather to skid in broadside in a cloud of smoke, thoroughly used up, totally worn out, and loudly proclaiming "Wow! What a Ride!"
~Hunter S. Thompson

"Nothing in the universe can stop you from letting go and starting over."
~Guy Finley

"You can't change how people feel about you, so don't try. Just live your life and be happy."
~Unknown

"What comes easy won't always last. And what will last, will not always come easy."
~Unknown

"Your value doesn't decrease based on someone else's inability to see your worth."
~Unknown

"Love isn't supposed to be easy; it's supposed to be worth it."
~Unknown

"Your flaws are perfect for the heart that is meant to love you."
~Unknown

"Don't hold someone for the sins of their past if they show that they will work for the future."
~Unknown

"Love is like a trap. When it appears, we see only light, not its shadows."
~Pilar

"Love can consign us to hell or to paradise."
~Pilar

"It takes a huge effort to free yourself from memory."
~Paulo Coelho

"When someone leaves, it's because someone else is about to arrive."
~Paulo Coelho

"Human beings can withstand a week without water, two weeks without food, many years of homelessness, but not loneliness. It is the worst of all tortures, the worst of all sufferings."
~Paulo Coelho

"Imagine a news story for your life and start living it."
~Paulo Coelho

"Life always waits for some crisis to occur before revealing itself at its most brilliant."
~Paulo Coelho

"When at a loss for the right word to say, try silence."
~Unknown

"If someone doesn't appreciate your presence, make them appreciate your absence."
~Anonymous

"Offer your hand, not your judgment."
~Anonymous

"Your life is your story. Write well, edit often."
~Susan Statham

"We do not remember days, we remember moments."
~Cesare Pavese

"Pain doesn't just show up in our lives for no reason. It's a sign that something in our lives needs to change."
~Mandy Hale

"Letting go doesn't mean you forget the person completely, it just means that you find a way to survive without them."
~Unknown

"Sometimes the thing we can't change ends up changing us."
~Unknown

"Don't waste words on people who deserve your silence. Sometimes the most powerful thing you can say is nothing at all."
~Mandy Hale

"Sometimes when the people you love hurt you the most, it's better to stay quiet. If your love wasn't enough, do you think your words will matter?"
~Unknown

"Everyone goes through tough times, no matter who you are. Keep pushing forward."
~Derek Jeter

"Sometimes walking away has nothing to do with weakness and everything to do with strength. We walk away not because we want others to realize our worth and value but because we finally realize our own."
~Unknown

"Some people are going to leave, but that's not the end of your story; that's the end of their part in your story."
~Unknown

"What you do in a heartbeat can last you a lifetime."
~Glenn Tarquinio

"There is a difference between giving up and knowing when you have had enough."
~Unknown

"There is no challenge more challenging than the challenge to improve yourself."
~Michael F. Staley

"People will come and go in your life, but the right ones will always stay."
~Unknown

"After having been in a couple of one-sided relationships, I now treat relationships like a 401k plan; I match what he puts in. If there is nothing to match, then it's time to move on to a better investment."
~Andrea Ziomek

"If someone wants to be a part of your life, they will make an effort to be in it. So don't bother reserving a space in your heart for a person who doesn't make an effort to stay."
~Unknown

"Those who don't understand your silence will never understand your words."
~Unknown

"You have the right to leave someone, but at least tell them why; because what's even more painful than being abandoned is knowing that you're not worth an explanation."
~Unknown

"How people treat you is their karma; how you react is yours."
~Wayne Dyer

"What you allow is what will continue."
~Unknown

"It's one of the greatest gifts you can give yourself, to forgive. Forgive everybody."
~Maya Angelou

"If you don't like something, change it. If you can't change it, change your attitude."
~Maya Angelou

"If you only have one smile in you, give it to the people you love."
~Maya Angelou

"You may not control all the events that happen to you, but you can decide not to be reduced by them."
~Maya Angelou

"There is no greater agony than bearing an untold story inside you."
~Maya Angelou

"Forgiveness means it finally becomes unimportant that you hit back."
~Anne Lamont

"When you chose to forgive those who have hurt you, you take away their power."
~Unknown

"A heart filled with anger has no room for love."
~Joan Lunden, *"Wake-Up Calls; Making the Most Out of Every Day"*

"The first step to forgiveness is the willingness to forgive."
~Marianne Williamson

"I eventually came to understand that in harboring the anger, the bitterness and the resentment towards those that had hurt me; I was giving the reins of control over to them. Forgiving was not about accepting their words and deeds. Forgiving was about letting go and moving on with my life. In doing so, I had finally set myself free."
~Isabel Lopez, "Isabel's Hand-Me-Down Dreams"

"Forgiveness is a gift you give yourself."
~Michele Weiner-Davis

"Holding on to anger, resentment and hurt only gives you tense muscles, a headache and a sore jaw from clenching your teeth. Forgiveness gives you back the laughter and the lightness in your life."
~Joan Lunden

"Without forgiveness there is no future."
~Desmond Tutu

"Forgiveness says you are giving another chance to a new beginning."
~Desmond Tutu

"The weak can never forgive. Forgiveness is the attribute of the strong."
~Mahatma Gandhi

"When you chose to forgive those who have hurt you, you take away their power."
~Unknown

"I hope someday that you find all my quotes, all my words and that you read them all. I hope you know that they're all about you."
~Unknown

The Guest House

This being human is a guest house.
Every morning a new arrival.
A joy, a depression, a meanness,
some momentary awareness comes
as an unexpected visitor.
Welcome and entertain them all!
Even if they're a crowd of sorrows,
who violently sweep your house
empty of its furniture,
still, treat each guest honorably.
He may be clearing you out
for some new delight.
The dark thought, the shame, the malice,
meet them at the door laughing,
and invite them in.
Be grateful for whoever comes,
because each has been sent
as a guide from above.

~Mewlana Jalauddin Ru

About The Authors:

Vincent Casale, a native New Yorker, joined the NYPD in 1984. Having spent most of his career on patrol and in Community Policing, Vincent experienced his fair share of domestic disputes. After his retirement, Vincent took on the role of "stay at home Dad" while his wife followed the career path of her dreams. Now a casualty of divorce, Vincent has experienced firsthand the financial turmoil that women endure during their divorce, often having to stay home, away from the workforce for several years. A single father of three, Vincent is a passionate writer and author of *The Coparazzi*. He is also a regular contributor to The Long Island Advance, a local newspaper in Nassau County, NY.

Dr. Thomas Billotti holds a PhD in Clinical Psychology and a Masters Degree in both School Psychology and Applied Psychology. During his 30+ year career as a private practice psychologist and school psychologist, Dr. Billotti has assisted countless children and adults through the divorce process. Dr. Billotti, a casualty of divorce himself, has experienced the emotional pain that divorce causes first hand and was witness to its impact on his children, as well as his relationship with them.

During his 30+ year career as police officer, Jayson Cole has witnessed the anguish and deep emotional pain of divorce countless times when responding to calls involving domestic disputes. Jayson, who has a deeply rooted passion to help others, describes what he learned from his encounters with casualties of divorce as a police officer and offers an intimate insight into his own, personal experience with divorce which resulted in parental alienation, devastating financial burden and the loss of valuable friendships. With the understanding that his emotional pain is shared by many, Jayson was able to make sense of the seemingly senseless and has successfully started to rebuild his life.

www.ingramcontent.com/pod-product-compliance
Lightning Source LLC
Chambersburg PA
CBHW061146040426
42445CB00013B/1574